BREAKTHROUGH BRIDGE

BREAKTHROUGH BRIDGE

Declarer Play for Beginners

Zia Mahmood and Audrey Grant

VIRGIN

First published in Great Britain in 1990 by
Virgin Books
26 Grand Union Centre
338 Ladbroke Grove
London W10 5AH

ISBN 0 352 32566 6

Phototypeset by Input Typesetting Ltd, London

Printed & bound in Great Britain by
Cox & Wyman Ltd, Reading, Berkshire

To those we love who are no longer with us.
To my brother Ali.
To L.B.

Contents

Foreword

I think it was just before filming *Lawrence of Arabia* that I first
discovered that 'finesse' didn't necessarily mean choosing the cor-
rect vintage of Dom Perignon. It was a discovery that changed
my life, as this introduction to the game of bridge, which
developed initially as a method of combating the frequent bore-
dom of film-making, changed to a passion and an involvement
that are stronger today than ever. It would be difficult to count
the hours of pleasure I have received from bridge, surely the most
fascinating of games ever invented, and I hope that you too can
derive the same joy after this introduction to the game.

Zia has long been a friend of mine and he is rated by many as
the No 1 player in the world. In my opinion, however, his contri-
bution has been much more than expertise because of the char-
isma and sense of fun that he brings with him to the game. He is
the living proof that bridge is not a boring game for boring people
but an exciting game that mixes all the most vital human qualities
and emotions.

In the *Breakthrough Bridge* series, Zia has combined his expertise and sense of humour with the talents of the internationally
known teacher and author Audrey Grant to bring an introduction
to the game that is essential for all beginners.

For once, you can learn the secrets of the game presented in a
simple yet entertaining manner that is as much fun to read as to
play. For once, you can actually listen to an expert as he talks
you through his thoughts on every basic step and situation. Finally, once you have read this book, I hope you will take up the
game of bridge as I once did, because I already know that its lure
is irresistible once felt, its addiction heady and exciting, and I
would like to share this knowledge.

Omar Sharif

Chapter 1

Introduction

'Lady Coote and Gerald Wade were amiable and discursive and the young man never failed to say at the conclusion of each hand, "I say, partner, you played that simply splendidly," in tones of simple admiration which Lady Coote found both novel and extremely soothing. They also held very good cards.'

From *The Seven Dials Mystery* by Agatha Christie

The play of the hand can be a high point in the game of bridge and many of us, like Lady Coote, find it extremely soothing when our partner notices that we played a hand well. After all, we are representing the partnership as the declarer when trying to take the number of tricks that we committed to in the auction. Taking tricks is what the game is all about. If the declarer takes enough tricks to fulfil the contract, his side collects points and if he is not successful, the opponents collect points. The play of the hand, or *declarer play*, is the focus of this book. We'll let you in on some of the secrets of the experts and show you the methods they use to get the most from the cards.

Making a plan

Since the declarer is responsible for both his own hand and the *dummy*'s hand, we will focus on his decisions. In this book, the declarer will always be sitting in the South position and the dummy will be in the North position. Before we get any further, though, we want to ask you a question. Since this is a book on play, let's get right to the point. You are playing in a contract of 2 NT, the opening lead is the ♠J. Which card would you play from the dummy on the first trick: the ♠A or the ♠Q? Here are the combined hands:

DUMMY
♠ A Q 2
♥ 8 6 4
♦ K J 3
♣ Q 10 6 3

OPENING LEAD
♠ J

YOUR HAND (DECLARER)
♠ 8 6 4 3
♥ 10 5
♦ A Q 7
♣ A K J 8

More important than whether you decide to play the ♠A or the ♠Q is the way you arrive at your decision. Before you choose the particular card to play in a specific suit, whether it is your first hand or whether you are a world-class player, you have to take a look at the big picture. You have to make a plan.

There are many different aspects to making a plan and many considerations. Most important is the concept that you have to stop and take a moment to decide how you are going to make your contract. The letters S T O P can be used to help remember the steps you go through on nearly every hand you play.

S — stop to consider your goal
T — tally your winners
O — organise your plan
P — put your plan into operation

Stop to consider your goal

The first step in playing a hand is to consider your goal. In other words, how many tricks do you need to take to make your contract? Does this sound too simple? It is the only way you can decide whether to play the ♠A or the ♠Q in the hand above. You are in 2 NT and so have set your sights on taking eight tricks.

2

Tally your winners

After you have stopped to consider your goal, the next step is to discover how close you are to getting there. Tally your winners. A winner, or a *sure trick*, is one you can take without giving up the lead to the opponents. Here are three examples to illustrate the point:

NORTH (DUMMY)
♥ 10 9 4

WEST
♥ Q J 6 5

EAST
♥ 8 7 2

SOUTH (DECLARER)
♥ A K 3

You have two tricks in this suit, one with the ♥A and another with the ♥K. You can take both of these tricks without giving up the lead to the opponents. Next, consider this example:

NORTH (DUMMY)
♥ 10 9 4

WEST
♥ A Q J 6

EAST
♥ 8 7 2

SOUTH (DECLARER)
♥ K 5 3

There are no sure tricks in this suit. There might have been a potential trick, if the ♥A were held by East. Then, you could lead a low card from the dummy and if East played the ♥A, you could play a low heart; if East played a low card, you could play the ♥K. Either way you would get one trick eventually. The way the cards are laid out in the example, however, the declarer is not entitled to a trick in the suit. The point is that the ♥K is not a sure trick.

Finally, how many sure tricks are there in this suit?

NORTH (DUMMY)
♥ K Q J

WEST
♥ 10 9 8 7

EAST
♥ A 6 5

SOUTH (DECLARER)
♥ 4 3 2

After the ♥A is *driven out*, the declarer will potentially be able to take two tricks. However, there are no sure tricks since, by definition, sure tricks refer to those you can take without giving up the lead to the opponents.

Three more ideas about sure tricks are worth noting. First, the declarer does not need to have all of the *high cards* in one hand. Each of the following examples has three sure tricks: one with the ace, one with the king and one with the queen.

1	**2**	**3**
DUMMY	DUMMY	DUMMY
Q 10 4	K 10 4	K Q 4
DECLARER	DECLARER	DECLARER
A K 3	A Q 3	A 10 3

Secondly, you cannot take any more sure tricks than the number of cards in the hand with the greater number of cards in the suit.

1	**2**	**3**
DUMMY	DUMMY	DUMMY
Q J	3 2	Q J 4
DECLARER	DECLARER	DECLARER
A K	A K	A K

In the first example, although you have the top four high cards, you can take only two sure tricks since both the declarer and the dummy each has only two cards in the suit. In the next example, although you have only two of the high cards, you still take two sure tricks. Those extra high cards in the first example did not do you any good because of the shortness in your hand and in the dummy. In the final example, you have the four top cards and can take three winners, since you have a three-card suit in the dummy. In order to take four sure tricks, either you or dummy would need to have a four-card suit.

Another consideration is that when the cards are unevenly divided between your hand and the dummy, you may have to play the cards in a certain order to enable you to collect all of your sure tricks. Take this example:

NORTH (DUMMY)
♦ K 4

SOUTH (DECLARER)
♦ A Q J 10 9 2

You have the six top cards: the ace, king, queen, jack, ten and nine. You have a six-card suit in your hand, so you can expect to take six tricks. The order in which you play the cards, however, can be important. If you play the ♦A and then a small diamond to the ♦K, you are in the dummy. You have no more diamonds left to get back over to your hand. If you can get there in another suit, fine, but this is not always the case. Play the suit again. This time play a small diamond over to the ♦K in the dummy. Next, play a low diamond over to the high cards in your hand. Now you can easily take all six tricks. The idea is to get to your *long side*. You want to get rid of the high card, the ♦K in the dummy, on the first trick so that it does not get in the way of your getting back to your hand. This is referred to as playing the high card from the *short side*.

Organise your plan

You want to look at the choices you have. In our sample hand at the beginning of the chapter, for example, you have the option of playing either the ♠A or the ♠Q on the first trick. The first two steps of your plan told you that you don't need any extra winners to make your 2 NT contract. Your goal is to take eight tricks and you have the eight sure tricks that you need. On this hand, you don't need to plan to consider ways of developing extra tricks.

Put your plan into operation

Only after you have gone through the first three steps of your plan are you ready to play a card to the first trick. Let's return to our original question: should you play the ♠A or the ♠Q on the first trick?

Stop to consider your goal
You are in a contract of 2 NT and so need to take eight tricks. Simple as that! Your goal is to take eight tricks.

Tally your winners
Remember that a winner is a trick that you take without giving up the lead to the opponents. Looking at the cards you hold in each suit, count your sure tricks as follows:

Spades	1 winner with the ♠A
Hearts	0 winners
Diamonds	3 winners with the ♦A, ♦K and ♦Q
Clubs	4 winners with the ♣A, ♣K, ♣Q and ♣J

The total is eight sure tricks. You have enough tricks to reach your goal.

Organise your plan

You have the option to play either the ♠Q or the ♠A on the first trick. Having gone through the first two steps, you know that you have the tricks you need. Therefore, you should take them. Your priorities are to take enough tricks to make your contract. By playing the ♠A you can do this. If you were to play the ♠Q, you may get an extra trick but you may also put the contract, unnecessarily, in jeopardy.

Put your plan into operation

Play the ♠A, not the ♠Q on the first trick, and then take your sure tricks.

Let's look at the entire hand:

Contract: 2 NT

NORTH
♠ A Q 2
♥ 8 6 4
♦ K J 3
♣ Q 10 6 3

WEST
♠ J 10 9 7
♥ A 7 3
♦ 6 4 2
♣ 5 4 2

EAST
♠ K 5
♥ K Q J 9 2
♦ 10 9 8 5
♣ 9 7

SOUTH
♠ 8 6 4 3
♥ 10 5
♦ A Q 7
♣ A K J 8

If you play the ♠Q on the first trick, East will win the trick with the ♠K and lead back a heart. The defenders can take one spade trick and five heart tricks to defeat your contract.

Let's look at this same hand again, making one small change. This time, you are in a contract of 3 NT. The lead is again the

♠J. The question remains the same: What do you play on the first trick: the ♠A or the ♠Q?

DUMMY
♠ A Q 2
♥ 8 6 4
♦ K J 3
♣ Q 10 6 3

OPENING LEAD
♠ J

YOUR HAND (DECLARER)
♠ 8 6 4 3
♥ 10 5
♦ A Q 7
♣ A K J 8

STOP

Stop to consider your goal
This time, in a contract of 3 NT, you need nine tricks.

Tally your winners
You still have eight winners.

Organise your plan
You need one more trick to make the contract. If you play the ♠A on the first trick, as you did in the first hand, you will take eight tricks, not enough to make 3 NT. Where can you develop an extra trick? None of the other suits provides an opportunity to get the extra winner you need. Your best chance to develop an extra trick is to play the ♠Q on the first trick and hope that East does not have the ♠K.

Put your plan into operation
Having gone through your plan, you can see that the only way of getting an extra trick is in spades. Play the ♠Q. This time, let's see what the opponents hold:

Contract: 3 NT

NORTH
♠ A Q 2
♥ 8 6 4
♦ K J 3
♣ Q 10 6 3

WEST
♠ K J 10 9
♥ A 7 3 2
♦ 6 4 2
♣ 5 4

EAST
♠ 7 5
♥ K Q J 9
♦ 10 9 8 5
♣ 9 7 2

SOUTH
♠ 8 6 4 3
♥ 10 5
♦ A Q 7
♣ A K J 8

The way the cards lie this time, by playing the ♠Q on the first trick you are able to take two spade tricks, three diamond tricks and four club tricks for a total of nine tricks. You meet your goal. Of course, you might have ended up taking only seven tricks if the opponents' cards were located as they were in the first hand, but you had no choice in a contract of 3 NT. You needed to take nine tricks. You are not risking your contract by playing the ♠Q because, if you don't take that chance, you can't take nine tricks. The point is that you don't want to take any unnecessary chances. In the first hand, you had enough tricks to make your contract and there was no need to jeopardise that by trying for an extra trick.

Summary

Before you decide what card to play on any particular trick, S T O P to consider the total picture. What is your goal? Tally your winners: how close are you to reaching your goal? Organise your plan: either to take your winners if you have enough to make the contract, or to develop a way of getting the extra winners you need. Finally, put the plan into operation. Only after you have gone through the first three steps of the plan should you play a card to the first trick.

Over Zia's shoulder

Let's watch Zia in action to see how even a world-class player has to STOP and make a plan before deciding on what card to play in a specific suit. At the end of each chapter, Zia will play three hands with you. Zia is always sitting in the South position so that you can look over his shoulder.

On each hand, we will give the auction first, along with any of Zia's comments. Then you can see the opening lead (boxed) and both your hand and the dummy. Examine the hand to see how you would plan to play it and then turn the page to see how Zia tackles the hand.

Here's our first hand:

Hand 1 Dealer: South

DUMMY
♠ K Q J
♥ A 6 4
♦ Q J 10
♣ 9 6 5 4

OPENING LEAD
♥ K

DECLARER (ZIA)
♠ A 10
♥ 5 3 2
♦ A K 8 3 2
♣ A K Q

NORTH	EAST	SOUTH	WEST
		(Zia)	
		2 NT	Pass
6 NT	Pass	Pass	Pass

On this first deal, I have dealt myself an attractive hand and we have ended up in my second favourite contract (especially playing rubber bridge). I am sure you know my favourite?

After an opening lead of the ♥K, I am pleased to see my partner's dummy and I am certainly planning to go through our S T O P procedure in such an important contract. How are we going to make our slam contract?

9

Solution to Hand 1:

Contract: 6 NT

NORTH
♠ K Q J
♥ A 6 4
♦ Q J 10
♣ 9 6 5 4

WEST
♠ 8 6 4 2
♥ K Q J 10 9
♦ 9 7
♣ 3 2

EAST
♠ 9 7 5 3
♥ 8 7
♦ 6 5 4
♣ J 10 8 7

SOUTH
♠ A 10
♥ 5 3 2
♦ A K 8 3 2
♣ A K Q

S   Stop to consider the goal.
     We need twelve tricks.

T   Tally the winners.
     This is a most enjoyable pastime:
       Spades   3 winners: ♠A, ♠K, ♠Q
       Hearts   1 winner: ♥A
       Diamonds   5 winners: ♦A, ♦K, ♦Q, ♦J, ♦10
       Clubs   3 winners: ♣A, ♣K, ♣Q

O   Organise the plan
     Well, it looks as if we don't need to develop extra tricks. As
     often does happen, we plan to take our sure tricks and make
     the contract.

P   Put the plan into operation.
     This time it is very simple. We show my hand to the
     opponents, pointing out our twelve top tricks (before I
     revoke) and claim the contract. Note that I still did not play
     to the first trick until I had gone through my mental exercise.

     Things are going well. We've made a slam, and we've only just
started playing!

Hand 2 Dealer: North

DUMMY
♠ K J 7 6
♥ K 6
♦ 6 5 4
♣ 7 5 3 2

OPENING LEAD
♥ Q

DECLARER (ZIA)
♠ A Q
♥ A 10 5 3
♦ A 8 3 2
♣ A K 6

NORTH	EAST	SOUTH (Zia)	WEST
Pass	Pass	2 NT	Pass
3 NT	Pass	Pass	Pass

It often happens that you get two powerful hands in a row. This time it is our partner who dealt such wonderful cards. Can we make two contracts in succession?

Solution to Hand 2:

Contract: 3 NT

NORTH
- ♠ K J 7 6
- ♥ K 6
- ♦ 6 5 4
- ♣ 7 5 3 2

WEST
- ♠ 10 9 8 2
- ♥ Q J 9 8 7
- ♦ Q 10
- ♣ 9 4

EAST
- ♠ 5 4 3
- ♥ 4 2
- ♦ K J 9 7
- ♣ Q J 10 8

SOUTH
- ♠ A Q
- ♥ A 10 5 3
- ♦ A 8 3 2
- ♣ A K 6

This is a very good hand to play together because it often catches those who don't remember to STOP before playing the first card.

S We need nine tricks.

T We tally our sure tricks.

Spades	4 winners:	the four top cards
Hearts	2 winners:	the ♥A and ♥K
Diamonds	1 winner:	the ♦A
Clubs	2 winners:	the ♣A and ♣K

O We organise our plan.
Since we have nine tricks, enough to make the contract provided we don't make any careless mistakes, we don't need to look for extra tricks. High cards in a suit are of no use unless we can get to them. The ♥K in the dummy is the way we can get to our good spades after we have played the two high cards from our hand. So, on the first trick, we can't play the ♥K. Instead we win the trick in our hand with the ♥A and play the two top spades. Now we use the ♥K to get over to the two good spades in the dummy.

P We put the plan into operation.
We play the ♥A on the first trick. Then we play the ♠A and the ♠Q. Now we get to the dummy with the ♥K and enjoy our two spade winners. We then take the rest of our sure tricks to make the contract.

Hand 3 Dealer: West

DUMMY
- ♠ K J 10 7
- ♥ A 8 5
- ♦ 6 5 3
- ♣ 10 4 3

OPENING LEAD:
♥ K

DECLARER (ZIA)
- ♠ A Q
- ♥ 9 6 2
- ♦ A 9 7 4
- ♣ A 8 5 2

NORTH	EAST	SOUTH (Zia)	WEST
			Pass
Pass	Pass	1 NT	Pass
Pass	Pass		

A quiet auction to a quiet contract. Nonetheless, we mustn't lose sight of our goal. Even a little hand like this can require some careful planning.

Solution to Hand 3:

Contract: 1 NT

NORTH
- ♠ K J 10 7
- ♥ A 8 5
- ♦ 6 5 3
- ♣ 10 4 3

WEST
- ♠ 6 5 3
- ♥ [K] Q J 10
- ♦ Q 10 8 2
- ♣ Q 7

EAST
- ♠ 9 8 4 2
- ♥ 7 4 3
- ♦ K J
- ♣ K J 9 6

SOUTH
- ♠ A Q
- ♥ 9 6 2
- ♦ A 9 7 4
- ♣ A 8 5 2

S Stop to consider the goal.
To make 1 NT, we need seven tricks.

T Tally the winners.

Spades	4 winners:	♠A, ♠K, ♠Q, ♠J
Hearts	1 winner:	♥A
Diamonds	1 winner:	♦A
Clubs	1 winner:	♣A

O Organise the plan.
We only require seven tricks this time and we appear to have the tricks we need. However, the lead of the ♥K has made our task more difficult. After we win a trick with the dummy's ♥A, it will not be so easy to take our four spade tricks. If we take the ♠A and ♠Q in our hand, how are we going to get across to dummy to take the ♠K and ♠J? Can you see what we have to do? The dummy's ♠10 gives us a way to end up taking four spade tricks. After playing the ♠A, we play the ♠Q and *overtake* it with the dummy's ♠K. It may seem wasteful to play two of our high cards on one trick but, on this hand, it is the only way we can get to the dummy. Now, we can take two more spade tricks, with the ♠J and ♠10.

P Put the plan into operation.
Win the ♥A, play the ♠A and then the ♠Q, overtaking

14

with the dummy's ♠K. Take the dummy's ♠J and ♠10 and then your ♦A and ♣A — and it's on to the next chapter. Well, if you made all three hands, you're well on your way to becoming a good declarer. If you didn't, maybe you'd like to come and play against me for money sometime!

Chapter 2

Promotion

Unsolicited advice at the bridge table should be avoided.

Sometimes you have the number of tricks you need and all you have to do is take them. Most of the time, however, when you compare your goal with the number of sure tricks you have, you find that in order to make your contract you have to develop extra tricks. One of the most untroubled options for finding extra tricks is through *promotion*.

Promoting winners

You can *promote* winners in a suit when you have a series, or *sequence*, of high cards. Consider this suit:

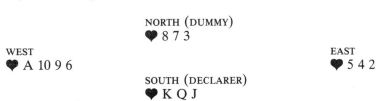

You have no sure tricks. Remember, a sure trick is one you can take without giving up the lead to the opponents. The suit does have potential for developing tricks, however. After you have played the suit and given the opponents the ace, you have promoted two winners. With this suit, you had only to give up the lead once. To take two tricks in this suit, you don't need to be concerned about how the opponents' cards are *divided* or which of your opponents holds the ♥A. They could be divided like this:

NORTH (DUMMY)
♥ 8 7 3

WEST
♥ 2

EAST
♥ A 10 9 6 5 4

SOUTH (DECLARER)
♥ K Q J

You would still be able to collect two tricks in the suit by giving up a trick to the opponents. Of course after you have taken your tricks, East would be a dangerous opponent, being ready to take three more tricks in the suit. Nevertheless, if you want to promote two tricks from this suit, all you have to do is drive out the ace. Let's look at another example:

NORTH (DUMMY)
♦ Q J 3 2

WEST
♦ A 6

EAST
♦ K 8 7

SOUTH (DECLARER)
♦ 10 9 5 4

Again, you have two potential winners. Only, this time, you have to give the lead up twice before you can enjoy them. Notice that the cards in the sequence do not all need to be in one hand. In the example above, the ♦Q and ♦J are in the dummy and the ♦10 and ♦9 are in declarer's hand.

There are times when you may have to give the lead up three times in order to promote your winners. Here is another layout:

NORTH (DUMMY)
♣ J 8 7 6 4

WEST
♣ A K

EAST
♣ Q 3 2

SOUTH (DECLARER)
♣ 10 9 5

There are two potential tricks in this suit, even though you would likely have to give the lead up three times in order to

17

promote them. This time, not only are the cards in the sequence divided between your hand and the dummy, but the suit is unevenly divided since the dummy has more cards than the declarer in the suit.

Getting to your winners

When the suit you are promoting is unevenly divided and there are more cards on one side of the table than the other, it is important to keep your eye on the long suit. Promoted winners are of no value unless you can get to them. Have you ever looked at winners on one side of the table which you can't get to? We certainly have. Although you can't call a taxi, with a little care you can provide yourself with the transport you need to get from one side of the table to the other. A means of getting from one side of the table to the other is called an *entry*. We'll be looking at entries throughout the book.

Promoting your winners in the correct order

When taking sure winners, it is important to play the high card from the short side so that a small card is left to get over to winners on your long side. When promoting winners you also need to play the cards in the right order. For example, you would like to promote five winners in this diamond suit:

NORTH (DUMMY)
◆ Q 4

WEST
◆ A 5 6

EAST
◆ 3 2

SOUTH (DECLARER)
◆ K J 10 9 8 7

Suppose you play the ◆K from your hand first and West does not play his ◆A. Next, you play a small diamond over to the ◆Q in the dummy. West still does not play his ◆A. You are in the dummy and need an entry to get back into your hand. You may have one entry in another suit. Suppose you use it to get back to your hand. Let's consider what has happened so far. Because West did not play his ◆A on either the first or second trick, you have taken two diamond tricks and have used one entry to your hand. You play a third round in the suit. West takes his ◆A. Diamonds have been played three times; you have taken

18

two tricks and the defenders have taken one. Three more winners have been promoted in the suit — if you can get to them. You need another high card to get back into your hand and you may not have one. You will never take the tricks you spent time promoting.

Play the suit again. This time, on the first trick play a small diamond from your hand toward the ♦Q in the dummy. West plays low. Lead a diamond over to a high card in your hand. Again, West plays low. You have now taken two diamond tricks and can lead a third diamond. This time West takes the ♦A. You have not used your one outside entry to play the diamonds so far and you have promoted three winners in your hand. Instead of needing two entries you need only the one to enjoy your promoted diamond winners.

Putting it into practice

It is important to watch your high cards in other suits. Keep the high cards with your long side of the suit in which you have to promote winners. After all, a winner is of no value unless you have some way to get to it. Let's look at a complete hand. The contract is 3 NT and the opening lead is the ♣Q:

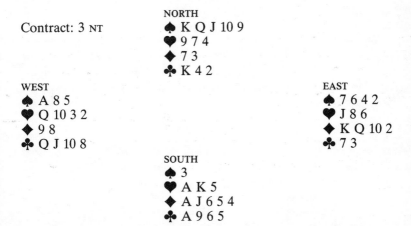

Contract: 3 NT

NORTH
♠ K Q J 10 9
♥ 9 7 4
♦ 7 3
♣ K 4 2

WEST
♠ A 8 5
♥ Q 10 3 2
♦ 9 8
♣ Q J 10 8

EAST
♠ 7 6 4 2
♥ J 8 6
♦ K Q 10 2
♣ 7 3

SOUTH
♠ 3
♥ A K 5
♦ A J 6 5 4
♣ A 9 6 5

What is your plan? Your goal is to take nine tricks. Your total winners are two heart tricks, one diamond trick and two club tricks — a total of five tricks. Organise your plan. You need to increase the number of winners by four so that you have enough

19

to make the contract. The four winners you need are available in the spade suit, after the ♠A has been driven out. You need that precious ♣K to stay in the dummy until your spades are established. Don't play it carelessly on the first trick. Your priority is to keep that entry with the long suit you are planning to promote.

You put your plan into action by taking the first trick in your hand with the ♣A and then playing your ♠3. Keep playing spades until the opponents take their ace. On this hand, West has to take it on the third round of the suit. The opponents lead another card. You don't care what it is. Suppose the opponents continue with the club suit. Take the trick with the ♣K in the dummy and enjoy your promoted spades.

It is horrible to contemplate, but what if you had played the ♣K on the first trick? You could play your spades and the opponents would win the trick with the ♠A. Now you would have no way of getting over to your promoted winners. Remember, you have two methods to help get your promoted winners. First, you can play the high card from the short side in the suit that you are promoting. Second, you can keep an entry in another suit — in this case it was the ♣K — on the same side of the table that has the length in the suit.

Summary

Extra tricks can be promoted when you have a sequence of cards in a suit by giving up the lead to the opponents and driving out the cards they hold which are higher than yours. This is a comfortable way of getting extra tricks. You don't need to be concerned about how the opponents' cards are divided. Your thoughts should focus on:

- Knowing how many times you have to give up the lead to promote your winners
- Playing the high card from the short side when the cards in the suit are unevenly divided to give yourself every chance to get to your promoted winners
- Observing the other suits so that you try to keep high cards with the long suit that you want to promote

Over Zia's Shoulder

Hand 1 Dealer: North

DUMMY
- ♠ A K 2
- ♥ Q J 9 2
- ♦ A 6 4
- ♣ K 4 2

OPENING LEAD:
♣ Q

DECLARER (ZIA)
- ♠ Q 4 3
- ♥ K 10 8
- ♦ 10 5 3 2
- ♣ A 5 3

NORTH	EAST	SOUTH	WEST
		(Zia)	
1 ♥	Pass	1 NT	Pass
2 NT	Pass	3 NT	Pass
Pass	Pass		

How should you and I proceed on this hand? I STOP — and so do you — to make my plan.

Solution to Hand 1:

Contract: 3 NT

NORTH
♠ A K 2
♥ Q J 9 2
♦ A 6 4
♣ K 4 2

WEST
♠ J 9 8
♥ A 7 6
♦ K J 9
♣ Q J 10 9

EAST
♠ 10 7 6 5
♥ 5 4 3
♦ Q 8 7
♣ 8 7 6

SOUTH
♠ Q 4 3
♥ K 10 8
♦ 10 5 3 2
♣ A 5 3

S   Our goal is to take nine tricks.

T   Let's tally our sure winners:

Spades	3 winners
Hearts	0 winners
Diamonds	1 winner
Clubs	2 winners

O   We organise our plan.
We need three more tricks and hearts seems a reasonable place to get them. By knocking out the ♥A, we would make three heart tricks. We have enough high cards in the dummy to be able to get to our promoted heart winners.

P   Put the plan into operation.
Now, and only now, can we play to the first trick. We win the ♣Q with the ♣A. Next we play the ♥K. No matter when West takes the ♥A, we end up with nine tricks.

Well played. Welcome to the world of bridge.

Hand 2 Dealer: South

DUMMY
- ♠ 9 8 7
- ♥ 9 8 6
- ♦ A 8
- ♣ K Q J 10 9

OPENING LEAD:
♦ Q

DECLARER (ZIA)
- ♠ A K 5
- ♥ Q J 10
- ♦ K 7 6 3
- ♣ 6 4 2

NORTH	EAST	SOUTH (Zia)	WEST
		1 NT	Pass
2 NT	Pass	Pass	Pass

Our partner is still 'bidding them up' and has tempted us to get dangerously high. But we have conservatively passed in a part-game. Thank you, partner. Nice clubs.

Solution to Hand 2:

Contract: 2 NT

NORTH
- ♠ 9 8 7
- ♥ 9 8 6
- ♦ A 8
- ♣ K Q J 10 9

WEST
- ♠ J 6 4
- ♥ K 7 3 2
- ♦ Q J 10 5
- ♣ 5 3

EAST
- ♠ Q 10 3 2
- ♥ A 5 4
- ♦ 9 4 2
- ♣ A 8 7

SOUTH
- ♠ A K 5
- ♥ Q J 10
- ♦ K 7 6 3
- ♣ 6 4 2

S   We need eight tricks to make our contract.

T   We have only four sure tricks: two spades and two diamonds.

O   We need four more tricks, and they certainly seem to be available in clubs. We could win the ♦A and play the ♣K. East could put on the ♣A and our suit would be promoted. But, as you know, the defenders aren't usually that kind. East may not play the ♣A until the third round. We will have taken two club tricks, but we have two more to take and we can't get to them. Fortunately we have the ♦K in our hand. So let's plan to win the first trick in our hand, leaving the ♦A in the dummy.

P   Having won the first trick with the ♦K, we can then play a club. Suppose East waits until the third round to take the ♣A. Although we have no clubs left in our hand to get over to the winners in the dummy, we do have that carefully preserved ♦A which will get us to the dummy and the promoted winners.

24

Hand 3 Dealer: East

DUMMY
- ♠ A K 6
- ♥ Q J 4
- ♦ 9 5 2
- ♣ J 10 9 4

OPENING LEAD:
♠ J

DECLARER (ZIA)
- ♠ Q 5 2
- ♥ K 7 3
- ♦ A K 10 4
- ♣ Q 7 3

NORTH	EAST	SOUTH (Zia)	WEST
	Pass	1 NT	Pass
2 NT	Pass	3 NT	Pass
Pass	Pass		

This time, we have enough to accept our partner's invitation to a game. Having bid a game, we still have to make it. It looks as though there is a lot of work to do. Where do we start?

Solution to Hand 3:

Contract: 3 NT

NORTH
- ♠ A K 6
- ♥ Q J 4
- ♦ 9 5 2
- ♣ J 10 9 4

WEST
- ♠ J 10 9 7
- ♥ 9 6 5 2
- ♦ J 7
- ♣ A 6 5

EAST
- ♠ 8 4 3
- ♥ A 10 8
- ♦ Q 8 6 3
- ♣ K 8 2

SOUTH
- ♠ Q 5 2
- ♥ K 7 3
- ♦ A K 10 4
- ♣ Q 7 3

S   We'll need nine tricks to make our contract of 3 NT.

T   We only have five sure tricks to start with: the three top spades and the two top diamonds.

O   With four more tricks to develop, we'll have to look at all our resources. In the heart suit, we can promote two extra tricks by driving out the ♥A. In the club suit, we can also develop two extra tricks but we'll have to drive out two of the opponents' high cards, the ♣A and ♣K. Where do we start? When there's a lot to do, it is usually best to start with the suit that requires the most work to develop — in this case, the clubs.

P   Win the first spade trick in either hand and play the ♣Q, starting with the high card from the short side. Assuming the opponents win the ♣K and lead another spade, win the trick and lead clubs again, driving out the opponents' ♣A and promoting two club winners. If the opponents lead another spade, we can win it and take our established club tricks. Now, it's time to go to work on the heart suit. Once we've driven out the ♥A, we'll have all the tricks we need to make the contract.

Hard work, but worthwhile — as we score up our game bonus.

Chapter 3

Tricks From Small Cards

In Toronto, a National Tournament was held in 1986 in which there were over 23,000 tables of bridge in play over a ten-day period.

Since there are only four face cards in each suit — the ace, king, queen and jack — it is important to develop techniques for turning small cards into winners. Does this sound like a magic trick? It can be done. Once the opponents have no cards left to play and cannot follow suit, a card as seemingly insignificant as a two can be as powerful as an ace.

Establishing tricks in long suits

Consider this suit:

NORTH (DUMMY)
♥ A K 3 2

WEST
♥ J 10 9

EAST
♥ 8 7

SOUTH (DECLARER)
♥ Q 6 5 4

You expect to take your three high cards, the ace, king and queen. By playing the suit three times, however, you have exhausted the opponents' supply of cards in the suit. Your ♥4 also becomes a winner. Look at the suit again. This time we'll change the *distribution*, or *division*, of the opponents' cards:

NORTH (DUMMY)
♥ A K 3 2

WEST
♥ J 10 9 8

EAST
♥ 7

SOUTH (DECLARER)
♥ Q 6 5 4

Your three top hearts are still winners. However, after you have played the suit three times, West still has a card left and it is higher than your ♥4. When the suit is divided like this, you are unable to develop an extra winner with your small card.

When you were promoting tricks through the force of your high cards, as we saw in the last chapter, you didn't need to consider how the opponents' cards were divided. Now, however, the division of the defenders' cards is important. You want to be able to predict how the opponents' cards are likely to be divided in order to feel comfortable trying to get extra tricks from the length in a suit. What can you expect on most hands? Is the suit more likely to be divided the way it was in the first layout or the second layout?

Considering the division of the opponents' cards

If the opponents have an odd number of cards in a suit, as they do when they hold five cards between them, the suit is likely to be divided as evenly as possible — that is, the way it was in the first example. When they are divided with three cards in one opponent's hand and two cards in the other opponent's hand, it is referred to as 3–2 distribution.

Now, suppose this is your suit:

NORTH (DUMMY)
♥ A K 3 2

SOUTH (DECLARER)
♥ Q 6 5

You have seven cards in the suit and the opponents have six cards, an even number. When the opponents have an even number of cards, they are likely to be divided unevenly. What does this mean? The six cards held by the defenders are likely to be divided so that there are four on one side and two on the other: 4–2 distribution, rather than 3–3. Look at two possible layouts:

1

NORTH (DUMMY)
♥ A K 3 2

WEST
♥ J 10 9 4

EAST
♥ 8 7

SOUTH (DECLARER)
♥ Q 6 5

2

NORTH (DUMMY)
♥ A K 3 2

WEST
♥ J 10 9

EAST
♥ 8 7 4

SOUTH (DECLARER)
♥ Q 6 5

Although you would like the cards to be divided as they are in the second example, 3–3, you cannot expect this to be the case. It is more likely that they will be divided 4–2 as in the first layout. Notice that we don't expect them to be divided very unevenly, 5–1 or 6–0, too frequently. Here is a chart of what you can expect:

EXPECTED DIVISION OF OPPONENTS' CARDS

Number of cards held	Most likely distribution
3	2–1
4	3–1
5	3–2
6	4–2
7	4–3
8	5–3

You don't need to memorise the chart. It is enough to notice the general concept: an even number of cards tends to divide unevenly, an uneven number of cards tends to divide evenly.

Getting to your winners

This time, we have a delightful suit to consider:

NORTH (DUMMY)
♠ A K Q 7 6

SOUTH (DECLARER)
♠ 4 3 2

You have eight spades and can expect the opponents' five cards, an odd number, to be divided 3–2. That means that if you play the suit three times, neither one of your opponents will have any cards left in the suit. You, on the other hand, will have two spades left in the dummy, which are winners. With this suit, then, you can expect to take five tricks. Let's look at the suit again and this time, we are going to make the layout more realistic. After all, you can't always wait to have such strength and length in a suit before you try to establish tricks with your small cards.

NORTH (DUMMY)
♠ A 9 8 7 6

SOUTH (DECLARER)
♠ K 3 2

After playing the suit three times, you still expect the opponents will have no cards left and that your remaining two small spades in the dummy will be winners. This time, however, you have to do a little work to get to this point. You play the suit three times, expecting to win two tricks — one with the ace in the dummy, the other with the king in your hand — and to lose one trick to the opponents. You have to lose one trick before your small cards are *established* as winners. Does it matter whether you take your two high cards and lose the third trick or whether you lose the first trick and then take your two high cards? It might well matter!

Winners which have been established in a suit are of no use unless you can get to them. If your only high card in the dummy is the ♠A, then you better save it until you are in a position to take your established winners. Consider what would happen if you won the first two tricks with the ace and king and gave up a trick. After the defenders take the third spade trick, you have two good spades in the dummy, but no way to get to them.

Now, try giving up the first trick to the opponents. The next time you get the lead, be careful. Play the high card from the short side, your ♣K, and then a small card over to your ♣A in the dummy. You are now in a position to enjoy the last two winners in the suit.

Putting it into practice

Let's look at the concept of developing tricks from small cards in a complete hand. The contract is 3 NT and the opening lead is the ♣Q.

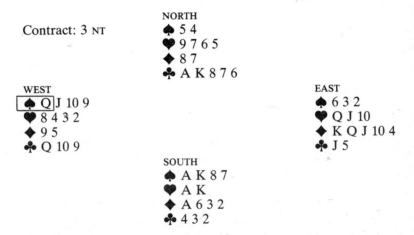

Contract: 3 NT

NORTH
♠ 5 4
♥ 9 7 6 5
♦ 8 7
♣ A K 8 7 6

WEST
♠ Q J 10 9
♥ 8 4 3 2
♦ 9 5
♣ Q 10 9

EAST
♠ 6 3 2
♥ Q J 10
♦ K Q J 10 4
♣ J 5

SOUTH
♠ A K 8 7
♥ A K
♦ A 6 3 2
♣ 4 3 2

Plan the play. You need nine tricks and have seven sure winners: two spades, two hearts, one diamond and two clubs. The two more tricks you need can best be developed in the club suit. You can expect the opponents' five cards in the suit to be divided 3–2 which means that after you play the suit three times, your two small clubs in the dummy will be winners.

Remember, you have to have transport to get to your winners. This would seem to be no problem at all. After all, you have both the ♣A and ♣K in the dummy. You do, however, have to play the suit three times, not twice, before those winners are established. If you play the ♣A and ♣K first, and then a third round of clubs, the defenders would take their trick. True, you have now exhausted their supply of clubs and have two winners in the dummy but you also have no way to get to them.

Instead, lose the first (or second) club trick. Now when you get the lead, you can play a small card over to your ♣A and ♣K and are in a position to take the next four tricks. You are not compelled to take your winners first. As a matter of fact, one of the bridge maxims is to take your losses early.

Giving up the lead

Before we leave the subject of long suits, it is important to notice that you might have to give up the lead not once, not twice but three times to establish a winner from your small cards:

NORTH (DUMMY)
♦ 8 7 6 4

SOUTH (DECLARER)
♦ 9 5 3 2

Is there any sense in giving a suit like this a second glance? The opponents have five cards in the suit, which you expect to be divided 3–2. If you could afford to give the lead up three times, you could eventually establish a winner in the suit. Let's hope you don't have to resort to this too often, but it is worth noticing that it could be done.

Summary

When you have a suit with eight or more combined cards, you should look to that suit as a source of tricks with your small cards, even if the suit is not headed by a bevy of honours.

Consider how you are going to get to your established winners. It might require giving up the lead early once or twice in order to preserve an ace until the small cards have been established.

Be prepared to give up the lead once, twice or even three times in order to establish a winner with a small card.

Expect that an odd number of cards held by the opponents, five for example, will be divided evenly — 3–2 rather than 4–1. Similarly, expect an even number of cards held by the opponents, six for example, to be divided unevenly — 4–2 rather than 3–3.

Over Zia's shoulder

Hand 1 Dealer: East

DUMMY
♠ K 8 7
♥ K Q 5
♦ 10 9 6 3
♣ 10 6 5

OPENING LEAD:
♠ Q

DECLARER (ZIA)
♠ A 6 4
♥ A 10 9
♦ A K 8 4
♣ A 9 4

NORTH	EAST	SOUTH (Zia)	WEST
	Pass	1 ♦	Pass
2 ♦	Pass	3 NT	Pass
Pass	Pass		

We are in the most frequently played contract in bridge, 3 NT, and not for the last time. Let's go through our steps again.

Solution to Hand 1:

Contract: 3 NT

NORTH
- ♠ K 8 7
- ♥ K Q 5
- ♦ 10 9 6 3
- ♣ 10 6 5

WEST
- ♠ Q J 10 9
- ♥ J 7 4
- ♦ J 5 2
- ♣ J 8 7

EAST
- ♠ 5 3 2
- ♥ 8 6 3 2
- ♦ Q 7
- ♣ K Q 3 2

SOUTH
- ♠ A 6 4
- ♥ A 10 9
- ♦ A K 8 4
- ♣ A 9 4

S   We have to take nine tricks. This should not be too much of a problem, but let's take a look.

T   Our tally gives us the following information. Our sure tricks are:

Spades	2 winners
Hearts	3 winners
Diamonds	2 winners
Clubs	1 winner

We have eight sure tricks and need one more to make our contract.

O   Organise a plan.
Then most obvious place for the extra trick is from our diamond suit. We can play the ♦A and ♦K and another diamond. We assume the suit breaks reasonably, 3–2, (which it does) and we can establish an extra diamond winner with our last small diamond.

P   Put the plan into operation.
We'll take the first trick with the ♠A in our hand or the ♠K in dummy and play the two top diamonds and a third diamond, which we lose. When we regain the lead, the small diamond is established for the ninth trick.

34

Hand 2 Dealer: North

DUMMY
♠ 9 8 5
♥ J 10 5
♦ Q 7
♣ K 9 6 3 2

OPENING LEAD:
♣ Q

DECLARER (ZIA)
♠ A K 7
♥ A K Q
♦ J 10 3 2
♣ A 7 4

NORTH	EAST	SOUTH	WEST
		(Zia)	
Pass	Pass	2 NT	Pass
3 NT	Pass	Pass	Pass

You can never really explain the pleasurable feeling of picking up a hand like the one we have on this deal. It may be luck, but it still feels great. Well, once we are over the euphoria, how do we continue?

Solution to Hand 2:

Contract: 3 NT

NORTH
- ♠ 9 8 5
- ♥ J 10 5
- ♦ Q 7
- ♣ K 9 6 3 2

WEST
- ♠ Q J 10 3 2
- ♥ 9 8 6
- ♦ A 9 6
- ♣ Q 8

EAST
- ♠ 6 4
- ♥ 7 4 3 2
- ♦ K 8 5 4
- ♣ J 10 5

SOUTH
- ♠ A K 7
- ♥ A K Q
- ♦ J 10 3 2
- ♣ A 7 4

S   Stopping to consider our goal tells us we need nine tricks. The opponents have started attacking spades which, for the moment, is fine — but not for too long. The opponents have goals too!

T   Tallying our winners gets us to a total of seven sure tricks: two spades, three hearts and two clubs.

O   Our natural instinct tells us the best place to go for honey (or tricks) to increase our tally is in the club suit. If, however, we were to play the ♣A and the ♣K and another, even though the clubs would be set up, we would have no entry to enjoy them. So, we need to watch our entry carefully.

P   After taking the opening spade lead with one of our high spades, we play the ♣A. Then we *duck* a club, playing low from both hands and letting the opponents have a club trick. Now, when we regain the lead, we hope — as you can see in the actual layout — that all of our remaining clubs are winners. We have a small club left in our hand to get to them.

Did you decide this by using your plan? If so, well done.

Hand 3 Dealer: North

DUMMY
- ♠ A 10 8
- ♥ A Q 2
- ♦ 9 8 7 5
- ♣ A K 9

OPENING LEAD:
♥ J

DECLARER (ZIA)
- ♠ K 9 7
- ♥ K 4 3
- ♦ 6 4 3 2
- ♣ Q 10 8

NORTH	EAST	SOUTH (Zia)	WEST
1 ♦	Pass	1 NT	Pass
2 NT	Pass	3 NT	Pass
Pass	Pass		

We have some way to go before we can make this contract — or do we?

Solution to Hand 3:

Contract: 3 NT

NORTH
- ♠ A 10 8
- ♥ A Q 2
- ♦ 9 8 7 5
- ♣ A K 9

WEST
- ♠ J 6 4 3
- ♥ J 10 9 8
- ♦ A Q 10
- ♣ J 2

EAST
- ♠ Q 5 2
- ♥ 7 6 5
- ♦ K J
- ♣ 7 6 5 4 3

SOUTH
- ♠ K 9 7
- ♥ K 4 3
- ♦ 6 4 3 2
- ♣ Q 10 8

S   Our goal is to take nine tricks.

T   Eight seem to be easily available: two spades, three hearts and three clubs. We need to concentrate on finding just one trick.

O   We have lots of strength in each suit and can afford to give up some tricks in order to create winners — how about that diamond suit? Even though we have no high honour cards in the suit, if we keep plugging away at it, we can finally get a trick from a small diamond. We have to hope that the diamonds break reasonably.

P   We win the first heart trick and lead a diamond. The opponents win and, let's say, they lead another heart. We lead another diamond. They win and lead a heart. We win and lead diamonds once more. West wins with the last high diamond and can take his established heart trick — after all, he worked hard to get it! But, whatever he leads next, we win and can take a trick with our established diamond winner.

More power to establishing those small cards!

38

Chapter 4

The Finesse

The vision of bridge, a cigar and a column of smoke curling up to a low-hung lamp is yesterday's picture. Many of the major bridge tournaments around the world are non-smoking.

Finesse is described in the dictionary as 'delicate manipulation'. Let's consider the meaning of the finesse as it applies to bridge and see how we can delicately manipulate the cards to take more tricks.

Finessing against the ace

A *finesse* refers to taking a trick with a card when the opponents hold a higher card. Here are some card combinations which illustrate the concept of the finesse. We'll assume that no cards have yet been played in the suit.

NORTH (DUMMY)
♦ K 4 3

SOUTH (DECLARER)
♦ 6 5 2

In spite of the fact that the opponents have the ♦A, you can try to take a trick with the ♦K by finessing against the ace. Your next question probably is, how are you going to try to take a trick with the king when the opponents have a higher card in the suit, the ace? If you were to play the ◆K, obviously your opponents would put on the ◆A. Therefore, in this example, the method of winning a trick with the king cannot be to lead the ◆K. Instead, play towards the king. Play a small diamond from your hand toward the ◆K in the dummy.

Taking a finesse is like trying to be tactful. Although you may want it to work all the time, you are not always successful. In bridge, this type of finesse is successful only half of the time. You are going to lead from your hand towards the king. The missing ace could be in one of two places:

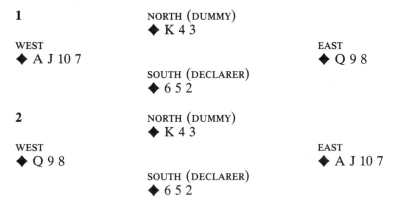

1

NORTH (DUMMY)
◆ K 4 3

WEST
◆ A J 10 7

EAST
◆ Q 9 8

SOUTH (DECLARER)
◆ 6 5 2

2

NORTH (DUMMY)
◆ K 4 3

WEST
◆ Q 9 8

EAST
◆ A J 10 7

SOUTH (DECLARER)
◆ 6 5 2

If the ◆A is held by West, as in the first layout, your finesse will be successful. Play a small card from your hand. If West plays the ◆A, your ◆K will be good on the next round of the suit. If West does not play the ◆A, your ◆K will win the trick on this round. On the other hand, in the second layout, when you play a small card, West plays a small card, you play your ◆K and East's ◆A wins the trick.

You are hoping that the missing ace will be in the position it is in the first example, with West. Isn't 50 per cent better than nothing? After all, if you were to lead the king, you are guaranteed to get no tricks in the suit.

Finessing against the king

By using the idea of the finesse, you can sometimes hope to take a trick with a queen when the opponents have the king. Consider this example:

NORTH (DUMMY)
♥ A Q 3

SOUTH (DECLARER)
♥ 5 4 2

You have one trick with the ♥A. In the first chapter, however, we saw that sometimes you also want to take a trick with the ♥Q. The general concept is that you lead towards the card you hope will win a trick — you can only hope, because you know that the opponents have the king. It is interesting that, when you were promoting winners, you were not concerned with the number of cards held by either opponent. When you were developing tricks with the small cards in your long suits, you were concerned with the division of the opponents' cards. This time you are interested in the *location* of the opponents' king. There are two possibilities. It is either held by East or West. Let's suppose West has it:

NORTH (DUMMY)
♥ A Q 3

WEST
♥ K J 10 9 8

EAST
♥ 7 6

SOUTH (DECLARER)
♥ 5 4 2

Play a small card toward the ace-queen combination in the dummy. If West plays the ♥K, take it with your ♥A and the ♥Q is a winner on the next trick. If West plays small, play — finesse — the ♥Q and it wins the trick. Of course, if East held the ♥K, you would not be successful in winning a trick with the ♥Q. A finesse like this is only successful half of the time.

The ace and queen do not have to be on the same side of the table:

NORTH (DUMMY)
♠ A 5 4

SOUTH (DECLARER)
♠ Q 3 2

You still hope the ♠Q will win a trick, so lead from the dummy towards the ♠Q in your hand. You are hoping that this is the layout of the opponents' cards:

NORTH (DUMMY)
♠ A 5 4

WEST
♠ J 10 9

EAST
♠ K 8 7 6

SOUTH (DECLARER)
♠ Q 3 2

Now, if East plays the ♠K when you play small from the dummy, your ♠Q is good on the next trick. If East plays low, your ♠Q will win this trick.

Leading the high card

There are times when you play a high card in the process of taking a finesse. Look at this example:

NORTH (DUMMY)
♣ A 9 8

SOUTH (DECLARER)
♣ Q J 10

The opponents have the ♣K, a higher card than the ♣Q, and yet you are hoping to successfully finesse against the ♣K and take a trick with the ♣Q. You would also like to take a trick with the ♣J or ♣10, making a total of three tricks in this suit. You want to prevent the opponents from winning a trick with their ♣K while you get your three tricks. The objective is to try to *trap* the opponents' ♣K. If that is your aim, let's consider how you would go about accomplishing it. Here is the entire layout you are hoping for:

NORTH (DUMMY)
♣ A 9 8

WEST
♣ K 6 5

EAST
♣ 7 4 3 2

SOUTH (DECLARER)
♣ Q J 10

In the previous examples, if you wanted to take a trick with a card when the opponents held a higher card, you played towards the card you hoped would take a trick. In this case, to trap the opponent's ♣K, you must lead one of your high cards. In order to distinguish when you can and when you cannot play a high card, ask yourself this question: how would I feel if the next opponent *covered* with a higher card? In the above example, play the ♣Q from your hand. How would you feel if West played the ♣K? That would be fine. You would take it with the ♣A and now your ♣J and ♣10 have been promoted into winners. If West did not cover your ♣Q with the ♣K, you would next lead the ♣J. Eventually, you would get three tricks in the suit, without losing any.

Do not confuse the example above with this situation:

NORTH (DUMMY)
♣ A 9 8

SOUTH (DECLARER)
♣ Q 3 2

Suppose you were to play the ♣Q and the opponent on your left covered with the ♣K. You could take the trick with the ♣A, but you would be no better off than if you had simply played the ♣A and put the ♣Q on the trick. You have promoted no extra winners, as you did in the previous example where you also held the ♣J and ♣10. By playing the ♣Q, you have given up a trick regardless of where the ♣K is located. If East rather than West has the ♣K, then he will take the trick with it when it is his turn to play. Either way, you do not get a trick with the ♣Q. Instead, play a small card from dummy towards the ♣Q. If the cards are located like this, your finesse will have been successful:

NORTH (DUMMY)
♣ A 9 8

WEST
♣ 10 7 5 4

EAST
♣ K J 6

SOUTH (DECLARER)
♣ Q 3 2

If East plays the ♣K, then your ♣Q is a winner on the next round. If East does not play the ♣K, then your ♣Q wins the first trick.

How can you decide when to play towards the high card you would like to win a trick and when to lead the high card? Look to the next trick. Ask yourself what will happen if your opponent covers your high card. Will you have gained anything? When you had the queen, jack and ten, you would gain something if the queen were covered. You would have promoted two winners, one with the jack and one with the ten. In the second example, where you have nothing to promote, you would gain nothing by leading the queen and would, in fact, have given up a chance to take a trick with it, since by leading towards it, you might have executed a successful finesse against the king.

Finessing against the queen

There are times when you want to take a trick with the jack when the opponents have the queen.

NORTH (DUMMY)
♥ A K J

SOUTH (DECLARER)
♥ 4 3 2

The idea is the same. Lead towards the card you hope will take a trick, the ♥J. Notice that you already have two sure tricks in the suit, the ♥A and ♥K. You hope that the layout of the opponents' cards is like this:

NORTH (DUMMY)
♥ A K J

WEST   EAST
♥ Q 10 9 8   ♥ 7 6 5

SOUTH (DECLARER)
♥ 4 3 2

Both of the high honours, the ace and king, do not need to be on the same side of the table. For example, the layout could be like this:

NORTH (DUMMY)
♥ A 4 3

SOUTH (DECLARER)
♥ K J 2

Now you are hoping that East holds the ♥Q. You would lead small from the dummy towards the ♥J in your hand; towards the card you hope will take a trick.

44

Repeating a finesse

There are times when you have more than one card you hope will take a trick. Consider this layout:

NORTH (DUMMY)
◆ K Q 4

SOUTH (DECLARER)
◆ 7 3 2

You might need to get two tricks from this suit, hoping to take tricks with both the ◆K and ◆Q. Lead towards the card or, in this case, cards which you hope will take tricks. The cards may be divided like this:

NORTH (DUMMY)
◆ K Q 4

WEST
◆ A J 10 9

EAST
◆ 8 6 5

SOUTH (DECLARER)
◆ 7 3 2

Lead towards your king-queen combination in the dummy. If West plays the ◆A, your ◆K and ◆Q will be winners on the next two tricks. If West plays low, you can win the first trick with one of your high cards and repeat the finesse against the ace. To do this, you would have to come back to your hand with a high card in another suit and then again lead low towards the honour you have left in the dummy. For example, suppose you played the ◆K on the first trick. This is what is left in the suit:

NORTH (DUMMY)
◆ Q 4

WEST
◆ A J 10

EAST
◆ 8 6

SOUTH (DECLARER)
◆ 7 3

Come back to your hand and lead another low card towards the ◆Q. If West plays the ◆A, your ◆Q is good on the next trick. If West plays low, your ◆Q will win this trick.

Putting it into practice

What opportunities for the finesse do you see in the following hand? The final contract is 3 NT and the opening lead is ♦2.

Contract: 3 NT

NORTH
♠ 6 5 4
♥ A 6 2
♦ J 3
♣ A 8 6 4 2

WEST
♠ Q 10 9
♥ 7 5 4 3
♦ K 8 5 2
♣ 9 5

EAST
♠ K J 7 2
♥ 10 8
♦ Q 10 9 4
♣ K J 10

SOUTH
♠ A 8 3
♥ K Q J 9
♦ A 7 6
♣ Q 7 3

Your goal is to take nine tricks. There is one sure spade trick, four hearts, one diamond and one club for a total of seven winners. Two more need to be developed. The opening lead is a diamond and you have the ♦A in your hand and ♦J in the dummy. You would like to win a trick with the ♦J but when you are missing both the king and the queen this is unlikely. Is there any possibility to develop extra tricks by finessing? Look at the clubs. You could hope to take a trick with the ♣Q by leading from the dummy toward your hand. Since you can see the opponents' cards, you can see that this is successful. You can develop one extra trick by finessing against the ♣K.

The other extra trick can be developed through the length in the club suit. This is what we talked about in the last chapter. You expect the opponents' five clubs to be divided 3–2. After you have played the suit three times, then, you have established two winners in the dummy. You still need to be able to get to your winners and the ♥A can be used as the entry you need.

Having organised your plan, it is time to put it into operation. After you win a trick with the ♦A, lead a small club to the ♣A in the dummy and then play a club from dummy towards the ♣Q in your hand. Suppose East plays low and you win the trick with the ♣Q. You have played the suit twice and won the first two

46

tricks. Lead the suit again, giving East a trick with his ♣K and establishing your remaining two small clubs in the dummy as winners. The opponents can now take the three diamond tricks they have established but, when you regain the lead there are enough winners to make the contract.

Summary

A finesse is an attempt to win a trick with a card when the opponents hold a higher card in the suit. In order to do this, you usually lead towards the card you believe could win the trick. You will be successful in your efforts about half of the time.

There are times when you have sufficient strength in the suit to plan to lead one of your high cards towards a higher card in the other hand in an attempt to trap one of the opponents' intervening high cards. You can tell whether or not leading the high card is a good idea by imagining how you would feel if your high card was covered by an opponent's higher card. If you don't mind, then go ahead and play the high card. If you can see that you have sacrificed a trick by playing a high card then the better idea would be to lead towards it.

There are times when you need to repeat a finesse, leading twice or more towards the cards which you hope will take tricks.

Over Zia's shoulder

Hand 1 Dealer: East

DUMMY
♠ 4 3 2
♥ 7 6 3
♦ 6 5 4 3
♣ A 9 5

OPENING LEAD:
♣ K

DECLARER (ZIA)
♠ 10 8 6
♥ A K Q J 10 9 8
♦ A Q
♣ J

NORTH	EAST	SOUTH (Zia)	WEST
	Pass	2 ♥	Pass
2 NT	Pass	3 ♥	Pass
4 ♥	Pass	Pass	Pass

I'm happy we're playing Acól and I can open a strong bid at the two level to show about eight playing tricks. This has encouraged my partner to bid on to a game with his ace and three-card trump support. In some systems, we might be languishing in 1 ♥. Having said that, I hope we can make the contract. Let's plan it together.

Solution to Hand 1:

Contract: 4 ♥

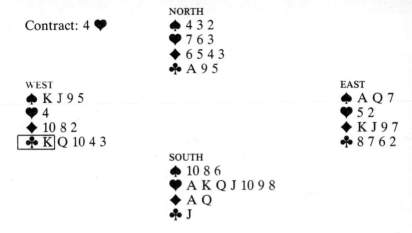

NORTH
♠ 4 3 2
♥ 7 6 3
♦ 6 5 4 3
♣ A 9 5

WEST
♠ K J 9 5
♥ 4
♦ 10 8 2
♣ K Q 10 4 3

EAST
♠ A Q 7
♥ 5 2
♦ K J 9 7
♣ 8 7 6 2

SOUTH
♠ 10 8 6
♥ A K Q J 10 9 8
♦ A Q
♣ J

S   Our goal is to take ten tricks.

T   We have seven heart tricks to go with the ♦A and ♣A, for a total of nine tricks.

O   The best chance for the extra trick we need is the diamond suit. If East has the ♦K, we should be able to get a trick with the ♦Q with the help of a finesse.

P   It looks normal to win the ♣A, draw trumps and then try the diamond finesse but, if I look closely as opposed to casually — which with my lazy nature is not so easy to do — I can see that I cannot get to the dummy in the heart suit because my hearts are too good. What will we do to get back to the dummy after the ♣A has been played on the first trick?

This is the kind of hand where we have to delay taking our trumps and try the finesse immediately, when we are in the dummy after winning the first trick. We use this opportunity to lead a small diamond and, when East plays a small diamond, play the ♦Q. As you can see in the full layout, this works and we chalk up another game.

Hand 2 Dealer: South

DUMMY
♠ 9 2 4
♥ 6 5 4
♦ A Q J
♣ K J 4 3

OPENING LEAD:
♠ J

DECLARER (ZIA)
♠ A K 3
♥ J 9 8
♦ 4 3 2
♣ A Q 9 6

NORTH	EAST	SOUTH	WEST
		(Zia)	
		1 NT	Pass
2 NT	Pass	3 NT	Pass
Pass	Pass		

For once West has not attacked our main weakness, the heart suit, but I am superstitious about feeling happy about anything until the hand is over. Let's make our plan.

Solution to Hand 2:

Contract: 3 NT

NORTH
- ♠ 9 2 4
- ♥ 6 5 4
- ♦ A Q J
- ♣ K J 4 3

WEST
- ♠ J 10 7 6
- ♥ A Q 7
- ♦ K 10 9 7
- ♣ 7 5

EAST
- ♠ Q 8 2
- ♥ K 10 3 2
- ♦ 8 6 5
- ♣ 10 8 2

SOUTH
- ♠ A K 3
- ♥ J 9 8
- ♦ 4 3 2
- ♣ A Q 9 6

S   We need to take nine tricks.

T   Our sure trick count brings us to seven top tricks: two spades, one diamond and four clubs.

O   The diamond holding looks really tempting and should be good for an extra trick or two. We can see that if West has the ♦K, by leading up to the ace-queen-jack combination, we can take three tricks. Whereas, leading the ace first and then playing the queen would promote one extra trick but would give the lead away unnecessarily whenever West does have the ♦K. It is always enjoyable to take a winning finesse and that is the answer here.

P   We win the opening lead with our ♠K in our hand and play a low diamond toward the dummy. If West plays the ♦K, we take the trick with the ♦A, and the ♦Q and ♦J are promoted into winners. If West plays low, we win the first trick with the ♦Q or ♦J. Now we come back to our hand to repeat the finesse.

Hand 3 Dealer: East

DUMMY
♠ A K 5
♥ A 5 4 3
♦ 5 4
♣ K J 4 3

OPENING LEAD:
♠ Q

DECLARER (ZIA)
♠ 8 7 6
♥ Q 7
♦ A 6 3 2
♣ A Q 10 2

NORTH	EAST	SOUTH	WEST
		(Zia)	
	Pass	1 NT	Pass
3 NT	Pass	Pass	Pass

My reputation in the bridge world for overbidding is well known, and in real life I get into a lot of dicey contracts. Luckily, Audrey has carefully selected the hands where she thinks I have bid reasonably normally — still, the play's the thing.

Solution to Hand 3:

Contract: 3 NT

NORTH
- ♠ A K 5
- ♥ A 5 4 3
- ♦ 5 4
- ♣ K J 4 3

WEST
- ♠ Q J 10 9
- ♥ 9 8 6
- ♦ Q 9 7
- ♣ 9 8 6

EAST
- ♠ 4 3 2
- ♥ K J 10 2
- ♦ K J 10 8
- ♣ 7 5

SOUTH
- ♠ 8 7 6
- ♥ Q 7
- ♦ A 6 3 2
- ♣ A Q 10 2

S   We need nine tricks to make 3 NT.

T   We have eight winners: two spades, one heart, one diamond and four clubs. Only one more trick needs to be developed.

O   There is a finesse against the ♥K although it doesn't look the same as those in the earlier hands. This time, the ace and the queen are in two different hands. Nevertheless, when we are in the dummy, we plan to lead a small heart towards the ♥Q, the card which we hope will take a trick. If East has the ♥K then we will get a trick with the ♥Q. Otherwise, too bad! There is nothing better to do on this hand.

P   So here goes. We win the first trick in dummy and lead a small heart. As you can see, Audrey has picked another hand where we are successful.

Chapter 5

Trump Contracts

If you can't play well, play fast. You will never be short of partners if you follow this advice.

Playing in a suit contract is, in many ways, similar to playing in a no-trump contract. The first step is to make a plan before playing a card to the first trick. When you compare your goal and your assets you may find you have all the tricks you need; all you have to do is to take them. As we saw in the first chapter, you still have to consider the best way of taking what you deserve. You may have to play a suit with more cards on one side than the other in the right order — the high card from the short side. You may have to remind yourself of your goal so that you are not tempted to jeopardise the contract in an attempt to get an extra trick which you don't need to make the contract. Other than that, it is quite straightforward. If you don't have the number of tricks you need, you could try to develop extra tricks by promoting winners in your solid sequences, by establishing the small cards in long suits, or by finessing against higher cards than you hold in a suit.

Playing in a suit contract, you also look to these tactics to develop extra tricks. Why then, you might ask, is there a separate section on play in a suit contract? We have seen that there are similarities between playing in no-trump and suit contracts. Let's now consider the differences.

Playing with a trump suit

The trump suit does have an effect on your priorities. You may have all the tricks you need, for example, and yet, if you don't play the trump suit first, you find one of your sure tricks might disappear to an opponent's small trump card. Here is an example. You are in a contract of 4 ♠ and the lead is the ♥K.

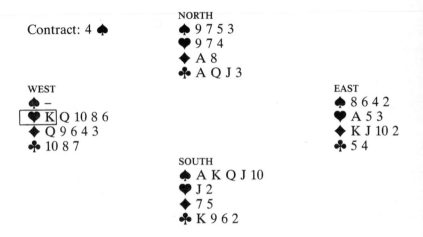

Contract: 4 ♠

NORTH
♠ 9 7 5 3
♥ 9 7 4
♦ A 8
♣ A Q J 3

WEST
♠ –
♥ K Q 10 8 6
♦ Q 9 6 4 3
♣ 10 8 7

EAST
♠ 8 6 4 2
♥ A 5 3
♦ K J 10 2
♣ 5 4

SOUTH
♠ A K Q J 10
♥ J 2
♦ 7 5
♣ K 9 6 2

You need ten tricks to make your 4 ♠ contract. You have five tricks in spades, one in diamonds and four in clubs, enough to make the contract. All you have to do is to take your tricks. Consider your priorities, however, taking into consideration the power of the trump suit. You will lose the first two heart tricks, but can take the third trick with a small trump card. What do you play next? If you decide to play the clubs, East can win the third round of clubs by trumping with a small spade. You had counted on taking all four clubs. You have given the opponents a chance to take a trick they didn't deserve. Now they can take the two hearts they started with, a diamond (after your ace is gone) and the small trump used to trump the third round of clubs.

If you have the number of tricks you need, you should *draw* the trumps first, by playing the trump suit until the opponents have none left. Don't give the opponents a chance to trump one of your winners. The trump suit does have an effect on the order in which you play the cards. In every hand you play in a trump contract, your first consideration is whether to play the trump first or to delay playing trump. We will go into this topic in more detail in Chapter 8.

Changing your point of view

The trump suit, as well as having an effect on the order in which you play your cards, affects the way you look at your hand. In a suit contract, it is better to consider your *losers* rather than your winners. Before we go into the mechanics of tallying your losers and the reasons for this change in perspective, it is important to remember that you are looking at the same cards. It's all a question of your point of view. Similarly, in a suit contract, we look at the hand from the point of view of the number of losers there are rather than the number of winners. It's all a matter of perspective.

Planning the play in a suit contract

Let's see how we use the letters S T O P to plan the play in a suit contract.

S: Stop to consider your goal

The first step in playing a hand in a trump contract is to consider your goal. How many losers can you afford and still make your contract? If you are in a contract of 4 ♥, you can afford three losers. In a contract of 6 ♦, you can afford only one loser.

T: Tally your losers

After you have stopped to consider your goal, the next step is to discover how close you are to getting there. Tally your losers. Focus on the declarer's hand and glance at the dummy to see if there is any help. At this point, you are not considering how to get rid of losers, only how to tally them. Consider this suit:

NORTH (DUMMY)
♥ 8 4 3 2

SOUTH (DECLARER)
♥ A K

How many losers do you have? None. Remember, you count losers from the *declarer's* point of view. Let's move the suit around:

NORTH (DUMMY)
♥ A K

SOUTH (DECLARER)
♥ 8 4 3 2

You appear to have four losers when you first look at your hand. By glancing at the dummy, however, you can see that the ♥A and the ♥K can take care of two of your losers. You are left with two losers in this suit. Now, consider this suit:

NORTH (DUMMY)
♠ K Q 3

SOUTH (DECLARER)
♠ J 10 2

You have three losers when you look only at your hand. Looking over at the dummy, and seeing the king and queen, you can see that you have only one loser, the ♠A.

O: Organise your plan

It is an advantage to count losers against a suit contract because you can use the benefit of the trump suit to help get rid of some of your losers. When you compare the number of losers you can afford to the number you have and find that you have too many losers, you want to organise a way to get rid of your extra losers.

There are two methods of getting rid of your losers in a suit contract that are not available in a no-trump contract. These methods are developed in more detail in the next two chapters, but here is the general idea.

One way of getting rid of losers in your hand is to trump them in the dummy. Consider, for a moment, the spade and heart suits in the two hands below. Spades are the trump suit and the hearts are a *side suit*. The clubs and diamonds are represented with X's since we are not focusing on them for the moment.

DUMMY
♠ 4 3 2
♥ –
♦ X X X X X
♣ X X X X X

DECLARER
♠ A K Q J 10
♥ 8 7 3
♦ X X X
♣ X X

If you were to count your winners in spades and hearts you would have five spade winners and no heart winners for a total of five tricks. Now let's look at the hand from the point of view of how many losers you have in each suit. Focus on the declarer's hand. You have no losers in the spade suit and three losers in the heart suit.

There would be no advantage to counting losers if there was nothing you could do about them. But you have a way of getting rid of your heart losers. You can use the three trump cards in the dummy to trump each of the heart losers in your hand and end up with eight tricks, or no losers. We will look further at this idea in the next chapter but, for now, you can see that by focusing on your losers in the above hand, you may be able to find a way to eliminate them to help make your contract.

If you were to focus on your losers in a no-trump contract — although you would not want to be playing in no-trump with the void in hearts on the above hand — there would be nothing you could do about your three heart losers. Not only that, but you might lose a lot more than three tricks in the suit since the opponents have ten hearts between them.

The second way that the declarer can get rid of the losers in his hand is to throw them on the dummy's extra winners. Again, you are looking for an unevenly divided side suit but, this time, instead of having fewer cards in the dummy than in your hand, you want to have more cards in the dummy than in your hand. Look at these hands where spades are the trump suit. This time, we'll focus on the clubs and diamonds:

DUMMY
♠ X X X
♥ X X X X
♦ K 8 7
♣ A K Q

DECLARER
♠ X X X X X
♥ X X X
♦ A 4 2
♣ 9 5

There is one diamond loser and no club losers. The clubs are unevenly divided between your hand and the dummy. On the third round of clubs you will have no clubs left to play and can discard another suit. You can throw away your diamond loser. Now, on the third round of diamonds, instead of giving the trick to the opponents, you can trump it, eliminating your loser.

P: Put your plan into operation
Once you have considered the number of losers you can afford, the number you have, and what you can do to diminish the losers you cannot afford, you are ready to play the hand. As in a no-trump contract, you never play your first card until you have gone through the steps of the plan.

Putting it into practice

Let's use the plan on the following hand. The contract is 4 ♥ and the opening lead is the ♣K:

Contract: 4 ♥

NORTH
♠ A 9 3
♥ 7 6 5 3
♦ A K Q
♣ 8 7 4

WEST
♠ 10 7 4
♥ A 4
♦ 9 7 5 3
♣ K Q J 10

EAST
♠ J 8 6 2
♥ K 2
♦ J 10 8 2
♣ 9 5 2

SOUTH
♠ K Q 5
♥ Q J 10 9 8
♦ 6 4
♣ A 6 3

Before playing your first card, go through the plan. Since the final contract is 4 ♥, the goal is to lose no more than three tricks. Next, total the number of losers you have. There are two heart losers, the ♥A and ♥K and, after the ♣A is played, you have two club losers left in your hand. That's four in total, one more than you can afford. If you were playing in a contract of 3 NT and were counting losers, there would be nothing you could do to get rid of them. You would have to lose the ♥A and ♥K along with three club tricks after your ♣A has been driven out, a total of five tricks for the defenders.

It is different in a trump contract. Because of the trump suit, there are ways of getting rid of the losers. Taking this hand as an example, focus on the club suit. You have three clubs on each side of the table. If you could get rid of one of the clubs on either side, you could trump the third round of clubs. There is extra help in the dummy in the diamond suit. On this hand, you could play your diamonds and, on the third round, throw a small club from your hand. Now, when the opponents try to take their club winners, you can trump the third round and lose only one club trick.

Timing is very important here. If you play the trump first, the opponents will get the lead and take their two club tricks to go along with their two top hearts to defeat the contract. Therefore, you have to get rid of the club loser on the extra diamond winner in the dummy before you give up the lead to the opponents. Once the club loser is eliminated, then you can draw the trump.

You can see that the decision to draw the trump right away or to wait until later in the hand depends upon your plan. You have to know how many losers you have and, more than that, you have to know the character of your losers. Are they immediate or slow? In the hand we just looked at, your losers were immediate and you had to get rid of them before you gave the lead up to the opponents. Since drawing trump would have given them the lead, that had to take second priority.

How can you know, then, when to draw the trump right away and when do you delay drawing trumps? We will look in more detail at your options in Chapter 8 but, for now, make your plan before playing the first card so that you know the number of losers you can afford and the number that you actually have. If you have too many losers, you may be able to get rid of one on an extra winner in the dummy as we saw on this hand.

Summary

The trump suit has an effect on the way you play a hand of bridge. Because of this, when you make your plan, focus on losers rather than winners. Stop to consider how many losers you can afford; that is your goal. Tally your losers, telling you how close you are to reaching your goal. Organise your plan. If you have the number of losers you can afford, start by drawing the opponents' trumps. If you have too many losers, plan on how to get rid of them and whether or not you can afford to draw trumps first. In a suit contract, in addition to all the techniques available in no-trump, you can trump losers in the dummy or throw them away on extra winners in the dummy. Finally, having decided on your plan, put it into operation.

Over Zia's shoulder

Hand 1 Dealer: West

DUMMY
♠ A 8 6
♥ J 10 3 2
♦ 10 9 6
♣ J 6 5

OPENING LEAD:
♠ 9

DECLARER (ZIA)
♠ K Q J
♥ A K Q 6 5 4
♦ 8 7
♣ 10 9

NORTH	EAST	SOUTH (Zia)	WEST
			Pass
Pass	Pass	1 ♥	Pass
2 ♥	Pass	3 ♥	Pass
Pass	Pass		

Oops! I hope we haven't got too high by trying for a game. Well, we're playing a trump contract this time. We'll have to change our focus and look at the hand from the point of view of our losers.

Solution to Hand 1:

Contract: 3 ♥

NORTH
- ♠ A 8 6
- ♥ J 10 3 2
- ♦ 10 9 6
- ♣ J 6 5

WEST
- ♠ 9 5
- ♥ 9 7
- ♦ A Q 3 2
- ♣ K 8 7 3 2

EAST
- ♠ 10 7 4 3 2
- ♥ 8
- ♦ K J 5 4
- ♣ A Q 4

SOUTH
- ♠ K Q J
- ♥ A K Q 6 5 4
- ♦ 8 7
- ♣ 10 9

S   In a contract of 3 ♥, we can afford four losers.

T   Our tally tells us that we have no losers in either spades or hearts, two in diamonds and two in clubs. That is exactly what we can afford.

O   All we need to do is win the first trick and draw the opponents' trumps before they can trump any of our winners.

P   Bridge is an easy game, isn't it? Did you notice how we still went through the steps of our plan before playing our first card?

Hand 2 Dealer: East

DUMMY
- ♠ Q J 10 2
- ♥ K 5 4
- ♦ K Q J
- ♣ J 10 2

OPENING LEAD:
♥ A

DECLARER (ZIA)
- ♠ A K 9 4 3
- ♥ Q J 7
- ♦ A 2
- ♣ 9 8 3

NORTH	EAST	SOUTH (Zia)	WEST
	Pass	1 ♠	Pass
4 ♠	Pass	Pass	Pass

West leads the ♥A and another heart. What's happened here? West seems to have made a rare mistake. It looks as if we had three clubs and one heart loser but now we have a chance. How do we continue?

Solution to Hand 2:

Contract: 4 ♠

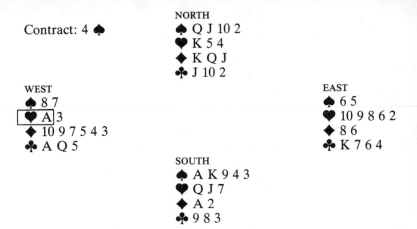

NORTH
- ♠ Q J 10 2
- ♥ K 5 4
- ♦ K Q J
- ♣ J 10 2

WEST
- ♠ 8 7
- ♥ A 3
- ♦ 10 9 7 5 4 3
- ♣ A Q 5

EAST
- ♠ 6 5
- ♥ 10 9 8 6 2
- ♦ 8 6
- ♣ K 7 6 4

SOUTH
- ♠ A K 9 4 3
- ♥ Q J 7
- ♦ A 2
- ♣ 9 8 3

It is tempting to start to play immediately, having had a reprieve, to get rid of those losing clubs before the defence change their mind and decide to take their winners. But let's pause and look at our plan.

S We can afford three losers.

T We have one heart loser and three club losers, one too many.

O When we plan how to eliminate a loser we see that we have an opportunity to get rid of a club loser on one of the extra diamond tricks in the dummy. When you are in a trump contract, unless the trumps are needed for some other purpose, the number one priority is to draw the trump. You don't have to give up the lead to draw trumps on this hand, so it is safe to do so. After you have drawn the trump, then you can discard your club loser.

P Only after making your complete plan do you put it into operation. Notice that, if we had tried to play the diamonds first, East would have trumped the third round of diamonds. West was also waiting to trump the third round of hearts. By drawing trumps first, you didn't give the opponents the chance to take tricks with their small trump cards.

Hand 3 Dealer: North

DUMMY
♠ Q J 7 5
♥ K J 3
♦ 10 7 3
♣ 5 3 2

OPENING LEAD:
♦ A

DECLARER (ZIA)
♠ A K 10 9 8 6
♥ A 2
♦ 9 8 2
♣ A 4

NORTH	EAST	SOUTH (Zia)	WEST
Pass	Pass	1 ♠	Pass
2 ♠	Pass	4 ♠	Pass
Pass	Pass		

It looks as if we have our work cut out for us on this hand since the opponents are about to take the first three diamond tricks and we still have a club loser. Is there any hope?

Solution to Hand 3:

Contract: 4 ♠

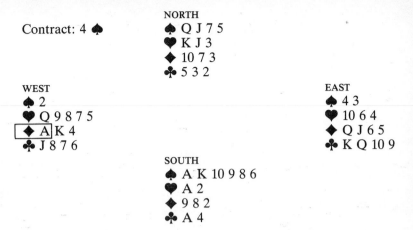

NORTH
♠ Q J 7 5
♥ K J 3
♦ 10 7 3
♣ 5 3 2

WEST
♠ 2
♥ Q 9 8 7 5
♦ A K 4
♣ J 8 7 6

EAST
♠ 4 3
♥ 10 6 4
♦ Q J 6 5
♣ K Q 10 9

SOUTH
♠ A K 10 9 8 6
♥ A 2
♦ 9 8 2
♣ A 4

S In 4 ♠, we can only afford to lose three tricks.

T The opponents take the first three diamond tricks and we might yet lose another trick, a club. That would be one too many.

O What can we do about our club loser? We can't trump it in dummy since the dummy has more clubs than we do. How about discarding it on an extra winner in the dummy? At the moment, there is no extra winner in the dummy but the hearts do offer some possibility. There is a 50 per cent chance that either opponent has a particular outstanding card and, if West has the ♥Q on this hand, we can get an extra trick by leading towards the dummy and finessing the ♥J. That would give us three heart tricks and we could dispose of our club loser. If the ♥Q is held by East, we won't make our contract. In fact, we'll probably be defeated by two tricks. But it is a small price to pay with a game on the line. They say you only live once.

P After the opponents take their three diamond tricks, suppose they lead a club. Win the ♣A and draw the outstanding trumps. Note that you can afford to draw the trumps first because you do not have to give up the lead while doing so. Now, it's time for the ♥A and the ♥2 towards the dummy. When West follows with a small heart, we play the dummy's ♥J and keep our fingers crossed.

Chapter 6

Trumping Losers

Remember that your partner is on your team.

The delightful aspect of counting losers is that there is a chance to get rid of them. In this chapter, we will focus on using the trumps in the dummy to get rid of losers in the declarer's hand. You can go through four simple steps when planning to get rid of losers in your hand by trumping them in the dummy. First, you have to recognise the hand patterns where the opportunity exists. Second, the trumps in the dummy have to be carefully handled. Third, you have to know that you might have to play the suit more than once, perhaps giving up the lead while doing it. Finally, you have to arrange transport, or entries, to your hand so that you are in a position to put the plan into action. Let's look at each of these steps in turn.

Recognising hand patterns

It is important to spot the characteristics in your hand and the dummy that offer the opportunity to trump losers in the dummy. The first step is to select a side suit in which there are more cards in your hand than there are in the dummy. Consider this hand. You are in a contract of 4 ♠ and the lead is the ♣Q:

DUMMY
♠ J 4 3 2
♥ –
♦ A 9 8 7
♣ K 8 7 4 2

OPENING LEAD:
♣ Q

DECLARER
♠ A K Q 10 5
♥ 10 9 4
♦ K 3
♣ A 6 3

There are more hearts in your hand than there are in the dummy and so the heart suit offers a chance to get rid of losers by trumping them in the dummy. You can play a heart from your hand and, since the dummy is void, you can trump it. Then you can come back to your hand in another suit and again lead a heart, which you trump in dummy. If you come back to your hand a third time and play your final heart which you trump in the dummy, you will have disposed of all of your heart losers in your hand by trumping them in the dummy.

Here are three other possible layouts for the heart suit. Which ones offer a chance to trump a loser in the dummy?

1	2	3
DUMMY	DUMMY	DUMMY
♥ 9 8	♥ K	♥ 9 8 6 4
DECLARER	DECLARER	DECLARER
♥ A 4 3	♥ 9 4 2	♥ A K

In the first example, you have three cards in your hand and only two in the dummy, so there is an opportunity to trump a loser in the dummy. In the second example, there are again more hearts in your hand than there are in the dummy, so you have the chance to trump losers in the dummy. In the third example, however, there are more hearts in the dummy than there are in your hand. This is not the pattern that gives you a chance to trump losers in the dummy.

Handling the trump in the dummy

It seems obvious, but the only way you can trump losers in the dummy is to have some trumps in the dummy to do the job. If you have a lot of trumps in the dummy, this will usually not present a problem. On many hands, however, your trumps have to be carefully handled in order to preserve the number of the dummy's trumps you need to take care of the losers in your hand. Consider the following example. We'll focus on only two suits: the trump suit, spades, and a side suit, hearts.

DUMMY
♠ 4 3
♥ —
♦ X X X X X
♣ X X X X X X

DECLARER
♠ A K Q J 10 9
♥ 9 8
♦ X X X
♣ X X

Count the losers in hearts and spades, concentrating on your hand. There are no losers in spades and there are two losers in hearts. Since the dummy has no hearts, the small trump cards can be used to take care of your heart losers. Now, decide how many trumps you will need to take care of your losers. In this example, you need both of the trumps in the dummy. You cannot draw even one round of trump. Your first priority has to be to get rid of your heart losers.

You plan to play a heart from your hand and trump it in the dummy. That will eliminate one heart loser and use up one of dummy's trump cards. You then need to get back to your hand to repeat the process, but you cannot do it with a spade. The remaining spade in the dummy is needed to take care of your second heart loser. You can't have your cake and eat it too. You will have to find another way to get back into your hand. Let's assume that you have an entry in another suit enabling you to get back to your hand. You can then play your remaining heart and trump it in the dummy.

By using your trump cards in the dummy separately, you get rid of both losers. You end up taking eight tricks — the six high spades in your hand will all take tricks and you get two tricks with the small spades in the dummy. Notice that you trumped losers in the dummy, not in your hand, in order to get the extra tricks. How many trumps would you need in the dummy to take care of the losers in your hand in each of the following side suits?

1	**2**	**3**
DUMMY	DUMMY	DUMMY
♦ 8	♦ 9 6	♦ –
DECLARER	DECLARER	DECLARER
♦ A 9 4	♦ A K 4 2	♦ 9 7 6 3

In the first example, you have two more cards in the diamond suit in your hand than you have in the dummy so you would need two of dummy's trumps to take care of the losers. In the next example, you have two more cards in your hand than in the dummy and so again you would need two of the dummy's trumps to take care of the losers. In the final example, you would need four of the dummy's trumps to take care of all four of your losers. You can see that you may not always have enough trumps to do the job. In the next chapter, we'll look at another way of getting rid of losers in case you can't trump them in the dummy.

Trumping in the declarer's hand

Let's change the layout of the suits from our earlier example:

DUMMY
♠ 4 3
♥ 7 6 5
♦ X X X X
♣ X X X X

DECLARER
♠ A K Q J 10 9
♥ –
♦ X X X X
♣ X X X

In your hand, you have no losers in spades or hearts losers. If you were to play a heart from the dummy and trump it in your hand, you would gain nothing since you would be using a trump which you had already counted as a winner. You only gain tricks when you are able to trump losers in the hand with the shorter trumps, which is usually the dummy. You can avoid thinking you are getting extra tricks by trumping in the long side, in this case in your hand, by focusing on the hand pattern. Since you do not have more cards in the heart suit in your hand than are in the dummy, this is not the pattern you are looking for. Look for hand patterns in which the declarer has more cards in a side suit than there are in the dummy.

Getting ready to trump losers in the dummy

It is convenient to have a void in the dummy when you are planning to trump losers, but this won't always be the case. Sometimes you have to do a little work to create the void in dummy. Again, let's focus on a hand where spades are trump and hearts are one of your side suits:

DUMMY
♠ 4 3 2
♥ 7
♦ X X X X
♣ X X X X X

DECLARER
♠ A K Q J 10 9
♥ 9 8 6
♦ X X
♣ X X

You have no spade losers and three heart losers. When you look to the dummy, you can see an opportunity to get rid of two, not three, of your heart losers by trumping them. You will need two spades in the dummy to trump your losing hearts. You will also have to lose a heart trick before the dummy has a heart void and you are in a position to trump your losers.

What are your priorities? How are you going to handle your trumps? Should you draw one round of trumps? You only need two spades to take care of your losing hearts. Look at what might happen if you decide to draw one round of trumps. You are still left with two spades in the dummy, which may seem to be enough . . . if you didn't have opponents. When you give up a heart trick to the opponents, they may lead a spade, leaving you with only one spade in the dummy and two heart losers in your hand.

72

Don't take that chance. Your first consideration is to get rid of your heart losers, so first play the heart suit right away. The opponents may lead a spade but you can win the trick and still have two spades left in the dummy. Play a heart and trump it. Come back to your hand in another suit and play your third heart and trump it. You will take the six trump tricks in your hand and two trumps in the dummy which you used on your heart suit. Now, let's take this idea one step further.

DUMMY
♠ 4 3 2
♥ 7 5
♦ X X X X
♣ X X X X

DECLARER
♠ A K Q J 10 9
♥ 9 8 6
♦ X X
♣ X X

Again, you have three heart losers in your hand. Is there any opportunity to get rid of them? You could get rid of one heart loser after the two hearts have been played from the dummy. How many trumps do you need? Only one. Whenever you are in a trump contract, the priority of drawing the opponents' trump cards should be on your mind. Should this be a priority in this hand? After all, you need only one trump card this time to take care of the heart loser.

Consider what would happen if you drew even one round of trumps. You would have only two spades left in the dummy and you have to give up the lead twice before you are in a position to trump your heart loser. Both times the opponents get the lead, they could play a trump, removing your last two trump cards before you could use them on your heart loser. It is important, then, to play a heart before touching the trumps, even once. If the defenders lead trumps each time they get the lead, they will only be able to take two rounds and you would still have one left to take care of your final heart.

The opportunity to trump a loser in the dummy exists whenever the declarer has more cards in the suit than the dummy. If the declarer has cards in the suit and the dummy has a void, there is an immediate opportunity to trump losers. Most of the time, however, the declarer has to play the suit, once, twice or more, in order to create the void so that one of the dummy's small trumps can be used. Let's look at a complete hand. You are in a partgame contract of 2 ♠ and the opening lead is the ♥4.

Contract: 2 ♠

NORTH
♠ K Q 7
♥ 7 6 5 3
♦ Q 4 3 2
♣ 8 2

WEST
♠ 8 4
♥ K J 8 [4]
♦ J 9 7
♣ A J 6 3

EAST
♠ 5 3 2
♥ Q 9
♦ K 10 6 5
♣ K Q 9 4

SOUTH
♠ A J 10 9 6
♥ A 10 2
♦ A 8
♣ 10 7 5

Let's go through the plan. First our goal. In a contract of 2 ♠, we can afford five losers. We tally our losers. There is none in spades, two in hearts, one in diamonds and three in clubs. That totals six losers, one too many. The next step is to consider how we can eliminate one of our losers. The ♥4 is led and after our ♥A is gone, we have two losers. There does not seem to be the opportunity to get rid of a heart loser. Consider the diamonds. There are only two in our hand. Perhaps the queen in the dummy could win a trick but, as you can see on the actual layout of the cards, the ♦K could be held by East. It would do no good to trump one of the dummy's diamonds in our hand since that would not eliminate any losers. The pattern we are looking for is to have more cards in a side suit in our hand than we do in the dummy. In the diamond suit we have more diamonds in the dummy than we do in our hand. That leads us, finally, to the club suit.

Since there are more clubs in your hand than there are in the dummy, there is the opportunity to trump a club. First, however, you have to play two rounds of the suit so that there is a void in the dummy. Each time you give up the lead to the opponents while you are creating this void in the dummy, they can lead a spade. Since you have to give up the lead twice, they are able to play spades twice, leaving you with one left in the dummy. Notice that if you drew even one round of spades, you would run out of the trumps in the dummy needed to take care of the club loser. On this hand, your first priority is to play the clubs after winning the ♥A.

Preserving your entries

On to the last step to consider when trumping losers. You have seen that, in order to trump a loser in the dummy, you have to be in your hand to lead the loser that you plan to trump. This means that you may have to preserve entries back to your hand. First, look at the layout of this side suit:

DUMMY
♣ K 4

DECLARER
♣ A 6 3

You have more cards in the suit in your hand than in the dummy, so you have recognised the pattern for trumping losers in the dummy. You need one trump to take care of your losing club. You first have to play the clubs twice in order to get ready to trump in the dummy. Ask yourself which hand you would like to end up in after you have played two rounds of clubs. You want to end up in your hand, so that you can lead the third club and trump it in the dummy. So, win the first trick with the ♣K in the dummy and play the ♣4 back to your ♣A. Now you are in the right hand to play a third round of clubs.

Sometimes, the suit containing the losers may not provide the entry and you will have to look for an entry in another suit. You usually have a lot of high cards in the trump suit, but you may not be able to use the trump suit since you need your trumps. Suppose you are planning to trump a loser in this suit:

DUMMY
♣ 8 4

DECLARER
♣ 10 6 3

The first two times you play this suit, it does not matter which side of the table you are on. After the suit has been played twice, however, you want to be in your hand to play the third round.

You have to be careful to keep a high card in another side suit in your hand as a means of transport back to your hand.

Summary

The opportunity to trump losers in the dummy exists when the declarer has more cards in his hand in a side suit than in the dummy. You need to keep the appropriate number of trumps in the dummy to do the job. Sometimes the dummy has a void and the opportunity to trump a loser immediately exists. At other times, the declarer has to play the side suit once or twice until dummy has a void in the suit. The declarer has to keep an eye on the entries back to his hand and make sure there are enough to be able to get there so that he can lead the suit he wants to trump in the dummy.

Over Zia's shoulder

Hand 1 Dealer: South

DUMMY
♠ A 6 5 2
♥ Q 4 3 2
♦ A 7
♣ 6 4 2

OPENING LEAD:
♣ A

DECLARER (ZIA)
♠ K 8
♥ A K J 8 7
♦ K 4 3
♣ 7 5 3

NORTH	EAST	SOUTH (Zia)	WEST
		1 ♥	Pass
3 ♥	Pass	4 ♥	Pass
Pass	Pass		

This time we are going to STOP and make our plan with the focus on the losers, since we are playing in a suit contract.

Contract: 4 ♥

NORTH
♠ A 6 5 2
♥ Q 4 3 2
♦ A 7
♣ 6 4 2

WEST
♠ 10 9 7
♥ 10 9
♦ 10 9 8 2
♣ A K J 8

EAST
♠ Q J 4 3
♥ 6 5
♦ Q J 6 5
♣ Q 10 9

SOUTH
♠ K 8
♥ A K J 8 7
♦ K 4 3
♣ 7 5 3

S   We can afford only three losers.

T   We tally our losers and see that we could lose three club tricks — probably the first three tricks since the opponents have led a club — and a diamond trick.

O   Let's organise a plan to get rid of the diamond loser. We know our partner will not appreciate it if we don't make this contract after we accepted his invitation. The diamond loser could be eliminated by trumping the third diamond in the dummy. We will need one heart left after we draw trumps. If at all possible, drawing trumps is a priority. In this hand we have complete control since we don't have to give up the lead while accomplishing our task.

P   Let's put the plan into action. After the opponents get the first three club tricks they have to give us the lead. Now we draw the trumps, and on this hand that requires only two rounds of the suit since the opponents are divided 2–2. Then we play the diamonds by taking the ♦A, ♦K and trumping the third in the dummy. There's no problem left in taking the rest of the tricks.

Hand 2 Dealer: West

DUMMY
- ♠ K 6
- ♥ Q J 10 8
- ♦ J 7 6
- ♣ 10 7 4 3

OPENING LEAD:
♣ K

DECLARER (ZIA)
- ♠ A 7 5 4
- ♥ A K 9 7 6
- ♦ 9 8
- ♣ A 8

NORTH	EAST	SOUTH (Zia)	WEST
			Pass
Pass	Pass	1 ♥	Pass
2 ♥	Pass	3 ♥	Pass
4 ♥	Pass	Pass	Pass

We have been bidding in our usual aggressive manner, but considering we haven't gone down yet on any hand, let's continue with that style. This hand looks a bit harder, and West always seems to have an honour to lead!

Solution to Hand 2:

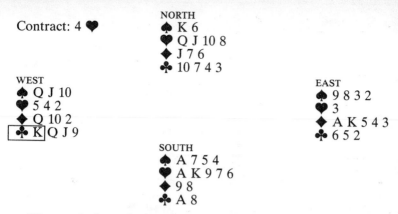

Contract: 4 ♥

NORTH
♠ K 6
♥ Q J 10 8
♦ J 7 6
♣ 10 7 4 3

WEST
♠ Q J 10
♥ 5 4 2
♦ Q 10 2
♣ K Q J 9

EAST
♠ 9 8 3 2
♥ 3
♦ A K 5 4 3
♣ 6 5 2

SOUTH
♠ A 7 5 4
♥ A K 9 7 6
♦ 9 8
♣ A 8

We stop before playing the first card; this hand isn't so easy.

S   We can afford three losers.

T   Our tally tells us that we have two spade losers, two diamond losers and a club loser — two too many.

O   We can plan to get rid of the two spade losers by trumping them in the dummy. Normally, after winning the first trick with the ♣A, we might consider drawing the trump. If they are divided 2–2, this would be fine. We could keep two trumps in the dummy to take care of the spade losers and could use our hearts to get back to our hand by trumping clubs. However, if the trumps are divided 3–1 or 4–0, we can't draw all of them. We cannot even afford to draw two rounds of trumps. Once our ♣A is driven out, we will have no way to get quickly back to our hand to trump the fourth spade. The opponents can lead a third round of trumps and down we go. We can only draw one round of trumps and must then start to trump our losers.

P   We win the ♣A and play one round of trumps, winning with the dummy's ♥Q. Then, we play the ♠K from the dummy which will win the trick and a small spade to the ♠A in our hand. We are in the right hand to trump our first spade loser. With two trumps left in dummy, we can use one of them to come back to our hand and now we can trump the second spade loser. We'll draw the opponent's remaining trump when we are next back in our hand. Task accomplished. Put the cards out and try drawing two rounds of trumps to see what happens.

Hand 3 Dealer: South

DUMMY
- ♠ A 6 4 2
- ♥ Q 8 2
- ♦ 10 5
- ♣ 9 7 6 3

OPENING LEAD:
♣ 5

DECLARER (ZIA)
- ♠ 9 7
- ♥ A K J 10 9
- ♦ J 9 4 2
- ♣ A 2

NORTH	EAST	SOUTH (Zia)	WEST
		1 ♥	Pass
1 ♠	Pass	2 ♦	Pass
2 ♥	Pass	Pass	Pass

This is not an unwelcome dummy in a modest 2 ♥ contract — but that doesn't mean we shouldn't give it our best. But just what is our best?

Solution to Hand 3:

Contract: 2 ♥

NORTH
♠ A 6 4 2
♥ Q 8 2
♦ 10 5
♣ 9 7 6 3

WEST
♠ K 8 3
♥ 5 4
♦ K 8 3
♣ K J 8 5 4

EAST
♠ Q J 10 5
♥ 7 6 3
♦ A Q 7 6
♣ Q 10

SOUTH
♠ 9 7
♥ A K J 10 9
♦ J 9 4 2
♣ A 2

S   We can afford five losers.

T   Our tally tells us we have a spade loser, four diamond losers and a club loser — a total of six, one too many.

O   Pausing after the opening lead (you did, didn't you?) and making a plan tells us that by simply playing on diamonds before the trumps, we can *ruff* at least one of our losing diamonds in the dummy. This is another case of delaying drawing trumps when there is something more urgent to do.

P   Win the ♣A and lead a diamond. Even if the opponents win and lead a trump, we can win and lead another diamond. They can lead a second trump but we win the race and can trump one of our diamond losers in the dummy.

Chapter 7

Discarding Losers

The Acol system, popular in Britain, got the name Acol because it was first played in 1934 in a bridge club in Acol Street in London.

In the last chapter, we saw that the declarer could get rid of losers by trumping them in the dummy. In this chapter, we are going to consider another way for the declarer to get rid of his losers. This time the extra strength in the dummy, rather than the shortness, is used to eliminate some of the losers in the declarer's hand. You can go through four steps when thinking about using the dummy's strength to get rid of your losers. First, you again have to recognise the hand patterns where the opportunity exists. Second, you may have to play a side suit several times before you can use it for throwing away a loser. Third, you may have to look for opportunities to create extra winners in the dummy through promotion, length in a suit or the finesse. Finally, you may have to arrange transport, or entries, to the dummy so that you are in a position to put the plan into action. Let's look at each of these steps in turn.

Recognising hand patterns

It is important to spot the characteristics in your hand and in the dummy that afford the opportunity to throw away losers from your hand on the dummy's extra strength. Look for a side suit in which there are more cards in the dummy than there are in your hand. This is the reverse of the pattern you wanted when you were trumping losers in the dummy, where you wanted more cards in your hand than in the dummy. After you have located a suit that is longer in the dummy, look to see whether there is enough strength in the suit to enable the dummy to win a trick while you are throwing away a loser from your hand. Consider this hand where spades are trumps.

DUMMY
♠ J 5 3
♥ A K Q
♦ 10 9 8 7
♣ A 4 2

OPENING LEAD:
♦ K

DECLARER
♠ A K Q 10 4 2
♥ —
♦ A 6 5 4
♣ 10 6 3

Find the suit with more cards in the dummy than in the declarer's hand. There are three hearts in the dummy and none in your hand. Next consider the strength of the heart suit. Since there are three winners, you can use this extra strength to get rid of three losers in your hand. After the opponents' trumps are drawn, you can cross to the dummy's ♣A and discard three of your losers on the hearts.

Here are three other possible layouts for the heart suit. Which ones offer a chance to throw away a loser from your hand on the dummy's extra strength?

1	2	3
DUMMY	DUMMY	DUMMY
♥ A K 9	♥ 4 2	♥ A K Q J
DECLARER	DECLARER	DECLARER
♥ 4 2	♥ A K Q	♥ 4 3 2

The pattern in the first example is worth looking at since there are more cards in the dummy than there are in your hand. There is not, however, the extra strength needed to throw away a loser. After the ♥A and ♥K are played, the opponents have the remaining winners in the suit. In the second example, there is the strength in the suit and the suit is unevenly divided, but you can not throw away a loser in your hand. The pattern you are looking for is one that has more cards in the dummy. The third example offers an opportunity to get rid of a loser from your hand. After the suit has been played three times, you have none left and can throw a card, a loser, from another suit. (Since the side suit has to be played so many times before you are in a position to get rid of a loser, it would be a good idea to first draw the trumps.)

Taking advantage of the dummy's extra winners

You are the declarer in a contract of 4 ♥ and count your losers in these two suits:

DUMMY
♦ A K Q
♣ 7 6 5

DECLARER
♦ 4
♣ A 8 3

In diamonds, you look to have one loser in your hand but a glance at the dummy shows that there is plenty of strength there to take care of it. You have two club losers. When you look to dummy's clubs, there is no help in the club suit. The diamonds, however, offer an opportunity for you to eliminate your club losers by throwing them on the second and third diamond trick.

You have taken advantage of a side suit that is unevenly divided between your hand and the dummy. When you were trumping a loser in the dummy, you wanted to work to eliminate all of dummy's cards in the side suit. When you are throwing away losers, you want to work toward getting rid of the declarer's cards in the suit. Here is another example:

DUMMY
♦ A K Q
♣ A 4 3

DECLARER
♦ 4 3
♣ K 8 7

You have two diamond losers in your hand but look to the dummy to see that the ♦A and ♦K can take care of them. The dummy's ♣A in combination with your ♣K eliminate two of the losers in that suit, but there is still one left. The diamonds offer a chance to eliminate your club loser. Play the three top diamonds and, on the third round, discard a club from your hand.

Whenever you are in a trump contract, look for opportunities to get rid of losers. Your first step is to identify side suits which are unevenly divided between your hand and the dummy. In the example above, the diamonds were unevenly divided. On the third round, because you had no diamonds left in your hand, you had an opportunity to discard a club, a loser in another suit.

Look at the effect this has. Now your clubs are no longer 3–3 and, when the third round is played, you are able to trump it, resulting in no losers in the club suit.

Developing extra winners in the dummy

There are times when there are more cards in the dummy than in your hand and, although there are not immediate winners, the suit offers possibilities. You can develop extra tricks in the dummy through promotion, length in a suit or by using the finesse.

Developing extra tricks through promotion
Let's look again at two side suits, clubs and diamonds. Hearts are trumps.

DUMMY
♦ K Q J
♣ A 4 3

DECLARER
♦ 4 3
♣ K 8 7

You have one diamond loser and one club loser. Consider what these two suits will look like if you lead a diamond to the dummy's ♦J to drive out the opponents' ♦A:

DUMMY
♦ K Q
♣ A 4 3

DECLARER
♦ 4
♣ K 8 7

85

Look for your unevenly divided side suit. There is an extra diamond in the dummy. Therefore when you play the suit for the third time, there will be a chance to discard a loser from another suit, your small club. Now, you end up with only one loser, the ♦A. This time, you had to promote your winners before they could be used to get rid of a loser.

Establishing a winner through length

We saw earlier on, when playing in no-trump contracts, that small cards can be established into winners when they are part of a long suit, preferably one headed by an honour or two. Consider this layout:

DUMMY
♦ A 8 7 6 5

DECLARER
♦ K 4 3

There are eight combined cards in the suit and the odds favour them being divided 3–2. That means that, after three rounds of the suit have been played, the dummy's remaining two small cards will be winners and the declarer will have no cards left in the suit.

There are other considerations when you are looking to your small cards for winners in the above layout. Because you can only throw away a loser on the fourth round of the suit, you would have to draw the opponents' small trumps so that they do not use them to win a trick by trumping an established winner. You also have to be able to get to the winners in the dummy. You might have an entry you can use in another suit or you may have to give up a trick early, keeping one of your high cards in the suit as an entry, as discussed in Chapter 3. Nevertheless, if you can turn those two small diamonds into winners, it is worth going through all those steps. Look at this idea in a complete hand. You are in a contract of 4 ♠ and the lead is the ♥Q:

♠ 8 4 2
♥ A 4 2
♦ 10 7
♣ A 5 4 3 2

OPENING LEAD:
♥ Q

DECLARER
♠ A K Q J 9
♥ 10 8 3
♦ A 6
♣ K 8 7

Go through the plan. You can afford three losers in a contract of 4 ♠. You have no spade losers, two heart losers, a diamond loser and a club loser. You want to eliminate one of your losers. What are your options? You don't have more cards in your hand than you do in the dummy in any side suit, so you cannot trump any losers in the dummy. Instead, look for the pattern to throw away losers. You have more clubs in the dummy than you do in your hand. Since there are two more clubs, you have a chance to throw away two losers.

After winning the first trick with the ♥A, draw the opponents' trumps. Next, take the ♣K and give up a club trick, leaving the ♣A in the dummy. What can the opponents do? They can take their two heart tricks but, whatever they lead next, you can win the trick. You can play your remaining club and win the trick with your carefully preserved ♣A. You are in the dummy and, if the suit has split the way you expect, 3–2, you are in a position to play one of your club winners and throw away your diamond loser.

Establishing a winner through the finesse
Another way of establishing an extra winner is through the finesse. Consider this example. Hearts are trumps and we are looking at two side suits, clubs and diamonds:

DUMMY
♦ A Q
♣ K 8 7

DECLARER
♦ 4
♣ A 4 2

You have a small diamond in your hand but the ♦A in the dummy will take care of that. You have one club loser after the ♣A and ♣K have been played. Where could you get rid of the club loser? Look to the diamonds, your unevenly divided suit. Although you don't have a sure winner, there is a possible winner with the ♦Q. Play your ♦4 towards the ace-queen combination. If your finesse against the ♦K is successful and the ♦Q wins the trick, you can play your ♦A and throw away a small club. Now you have only two clubs in your hand and when the suit is played the third time, you can trump.

It is important to look not only at the immediate chance to discard losers on the dummy's extra winners but also down the road to see what winners could be developed through promotion, length or the finesse.

Getting to the dummy

If you are planning on throwing away a loser on an extra winner in the dummy, you have to be sure to have an entry to the dummy. Let's look at one side suit, this time the spades, since hearts are trumps:

DUMMY
♠ K Q J

DECLARER
♠ 4

Once the ♠A has been played, you have two extra winners in the dummy, if you can get to them. You have to look to your other suits and try to preserve an entry so that, after the ♠A has been played, you have transport over to your promoted ♠Q and ♠J.

Summary

One way to get rid of a loser in a declarer's hand is to throw it on a winner in the dummy. You can recognise this opportunity by:

- Looking for a suit that has more cards in the dummy than in your hand
- Realising that you will probably have to play the side suit more than once before you are ready to throw a loser away.

Whenever possible, you will want to draw the opponents' trumps first

- Looking for opportunities to establish extra winners in the dummy through promotion, establishing small cards in long suits or the finesse
- Looking ahead so that you have an entry in the dummy to get to the winners when you are ready to discard your losers

Over Zia's shoulder

Hand 1 Dealer: North

DUMMY
♠ A 6 5 4
♥ 9 7 5
♦ 7 6 5
♣ K Q 8

OPENING LEAD:
♥ J

DECLARER (ZIA)
♠ K Q J 3 2
♥ A 6 4
♦ A 3 2
♣ A 7

NORTH	EAST	SOUTH (Zia)	WEST
Pass	Pass	1 ♠	Pass
2 ♠	Pass	4 ♠	Pass
Pass	Pass		

We can only afford three losers. Let's work together to see if we can hold ourselves to that number.

Solution to Hand 1:

Contract: 4 ♠

NORTH
♠ A 6 5 4
♥ 9 7 5
♦ 7 6 5
♣ K Q 8

WEST
♠ 8 7
♥ J 10 8 2
♦ J 10 4
♣ 10 9 4 3

EAST
♠ 10 9
♥ K Q 3
♦ K Q 9 8
♣ J 6 5 2

SOUTH
♠ K Q J 3 2
♥ A 6 4
♦ A 3 2
♣ A 7

S   Well, we decided we needed to lose no more than three tricks.

T   Our tally tells us that we could possibly lose two hearts and two diamonds.

O   What can we do? Is there any extra strength in the dummy that can be used? To recognise these opportunities we have to look for a side suit that has more tricks in the dummy than it does in our hand. The clubs fit that description. First, we plan to draw the trump; we have nothing to lose by doing that since we don't give up the lead and we don't need the trump suit for entries or to trump any losers from our hand.

P   Let's play the clubs carefully; first the ♣A, the high card from the short side, then the ♣7 over to the ♣K and ♣Q in the dummy. On the third round of clubs we can throw one of our losers, either a diamond or a heart. You choose, and we make yet another contract.

Hand 2 Dealer: East

DUMMY
- ♠ A K 7
- ♥ 8 7 3
- ♦ 7 3 2
- ♣ 10 8 6 5

OPENING LEAD:
♣ K

DECLARER (ZIA)
- ♠ Q 6
- ♥ A K Q 6 4 2
- ♦ A 6 5
- ♣ 9 7

NORTH	EAST	SOUTH (Zia)	WEST
	Pass	1 ♥	Pass
1 NT	Pass	3 ♥	Pass
4 ♥	Pass	Pass	Pass

Our partner has bid aggressively but we have reached a good contract. West always seems to have an easy lead! Let's play the hand.

Solution to Hand 2:

Contract: 4 ♥

NORTH
♠ A K 7
♥ 8 7 3
♦ 7 3 2
♣ 10 8 6 5

WEST
♠ 9 8 3 2
♥ J 10 5
♦ K J 10
♣ K Q J

EAST
♠ J 10 5 4
♥ 9
♦ Q 9 8 4
♣ A 4 3 2

SOUTH
♠ Q 6
♥ A K Q 6 4 2
♦ A 6 5
♣ 9 7

My immediate reaction is that I like the contract and expect to make it. So let's stop to make our plan.

S   We can afford three losers.

T   We have two diamond and two club losers, one too many.

O   Do we have any extra strength in the dummy? The ♠K will be an extra trick and can provide a good source to discard a loser. Should we draw trump first? A good idea. We don't have to give up the lead to the opponents, so they can't take any of their winners before we have a chance to get rid of our losers. Also we don't need the trumps in dummy on this hand.

P   There is one catch. Look at the spades. What would happen if you first lead the ♠A and play the ♠6 from your hand and then play the ♠7 from the dummy and win the trick with the ♠Q from your hand? Not pleasant, is it? In order to make the best of those spades, we have to play the high card from the short side and win the first trick with the ♠Q in our hand and then play a small spade to our winners in the dummy.

Hand 3 Dealer: East

                    DUMMY
                    ♠ 9 8 6 4
                    ♥ K Q 8
                    ♦ A 10 4
                    ♣ A 6 4

OPENING LEAD:
♣ K

                    DECLARER (ZIA)
                    ♠ A K Q 7 3
                    ♥ J 7
                    ♦ K 3 2
                    ♣ 7 5 3

NORTH	EAST	SOUTH	WEST
		(Zia)	
	Pass	1 ♠	Pass
4 ♠	Pass	Pass	Pass

The bidding is natural, simple and to the point. Can the play
be similar?

Solution to Hand 3:

Contract: 4 ♠

NORTH
♠ 9 8 6 4
♥ K Q 8
♦ A 10 4
♣ A 6 4

WEST
♠ J 5
♥ A 10 9 5 2
♦ 9 8 7
♣ K Q 10

EAST
♠ 10 2
♥ 6 4 3
♦ Q J 6 5
♣ J 9 8 2

SOUTH
♠ A K Q 7 3
♥ J 7
♦ K 3 2
♣ 7 5 3

S   We can afford only three losers.

T   Our tally tells us that we have a heart loser, a diamond loser and two club losers. One too many.

O   Before we go any further, look at the side suits that are unevenly divided. There are more hearts in the dummy than in our hand. Remember, it doesn't do much good to trump in our hand since we are trumping with a card we had already counted as a winner. To be effective, we should be trumping in the short hand. So, when there are more cards in the dummy than in our hand we are looking for an opportunity to throw away a loser. Does the heart suit offer that possibility? Maybe not on the first trick but, if we drive out the ♥A, we have two winners in the dummy and we could throw a loser on one of them, either a diamond or a club.

P   That's a good plan. So, we draw the trump — since there is no reason not to — and play the ♥J, starting with the high card from the short side. After the ♥A is driven out and we regain the lead, we can throw a loser on the promoted heart winner in the dummy — and we are fresh for a new challenge.

Chapter 8

Managing Trumps

Martina Navratilova says that no matter where she goes she can always make new friends at the bridge table.

There is a story that goes back to the days of playing whist, a forerunner of bridge. Whist was a gambling game, and the rumour was that there were hundreds of players who walked the streets of London, penniless, without food or lodging, because they failed to draw trumps. Apparently, like father like son (or like mother like daughter) and the story goes on to say that even the children of these players had to beg for a cup of coffee, all because they lost so much money at the gambling table due to their failure to draw trumps. When you first start to play bridge, one piece of advice that is often given is always to *draw trumps* before you do anything else.

Different countries have different sayings to remind you to draw trumps. In America, drawing trumps is referred to as 'getting the kiddies off the street'. When interviewing Zia in St Louis for my American television series, I asked him to discuss this maxim. He thought that we were talking about the drug problem in America — getting the children off the street — as compared with the drug problem in other countries. The producer of the show stopped us and asked that we try to keep to the topic of bridge. I had no idea why Zia was talking about the drug problem and he wondered why I wasn't sticking to bridge. The misunderstanding occurred because of the different idioms in each language. In

Pakistan, the maxim to remind you to draw the trump is 'pull the opponents' teeth out'. Well, bridge players all over the world are told stories or given maxims which essentially give the same advice. When you are in a trump contract, draw the trumps. Let's take a closer look at this advice.

One thing is certain. When you are playing in a suit contract, whether or not to lead trumps at your first opportunity is one of the decisions you have to make. You have several choices. You can lead trumps right away, extracting all of the opponents' cards in the suit; you can avoid drawing them altogether; you can compromise and play some trumps, then another suit; or, vice-versa, play another suit and then play trumps.

The guideline for drawing trumps does not come from an isolated rule like 'always draw trumps at your first chance' or 'save your trumps until you need them'. Instead, it comes as a result of making your plan. Before we go any further, let's consider what drawing trumps is all about.

Drawing trumps

Although the trump suit is more powerful than the other suits, and therefore unique, it also resembles the other suits. You go about playing the trump suit in much the same way that you would a side suit. You look for ways of promoting winners, you establish tricks in your long suit, you try finesses.

Usually your side has eight cards or more in the trump suit. If you have an eight-card fit, the opponents, therefore, have five cards in the suit, an odd number. You can expect them to be divided evenly between your opponents' hands, three on one side and two on the other, or 3–2. You would have to play the trump suit three times in order to get all the opponents' trump cards. If you have a nine-card fit, the opponents would have four cards, an even number. You expect them to be divided not 2–2 but 3–1. You still expect to have to draw trumps three times to remove the opponents' trump cards. Of course, there are no guarantees. When you have an eight-card fit, the opponents' cards could be divided 4–1 or 5–0, although that would be against the odds.

Sometimes, you can draw trumps without giving up the lead to the opponents and sometimes you have to give them the lead. Look at the difference between these two holdings in the trump suit:

1

♠ 9 7 6 4

WEST   EAST
♠ A K Q   ♠ J 10

DECLARER
♠ 8 5 3 2

2

DUMMY
♠ 10 6 4

WEST   EAST
♠ 9 7 3   ♠ 8 5

DECLARER
♠ A K Q J 2

In each case you have eight trump cards. In the first example, they are divided 4–4 between your hand and the dummy. If you were going to draw trumps you would have to play the suit three times and would lose the lead three times. In the second example, you would have to play the trump three times also, but you would not have to give up the lead even once to do so.

There are times when the trump suit is *solid*, as in the second example above, but, more frequently, your trump tricks have to be established through length as in the first example. You may also have to use the finesse when playing your trump suit. Consider this layout:

DUMMY
♥ Q 6 4

DECLARER
♥ A 8 7 5 2

You have an eight-card fit and expect the opponents' cards to be divided 3–2. You plan to play the suit three times to draw all their trumps. You have a winner with the ♥A. You can also hope to win a trick with the ♥Q. To finesse against the ♥K, lead towards the card you hope will take a trick. Lead from your hand towards the dummy's ♥Q.

Since the advice to draw trumps at your first opportunity is so often given, before we look at the exceptions let's consider why this advice is so popular. If a player cannot follow suit, a small trump card has more power than an honour card in the side suit led. Because of this, the declarer generally wants to get rid of the opponents' trump cards so that they will not be used against his winners.

Let's look at two hands where drawing trumps is a good idea. In the first hand, you are in a contract of 4 ♥. The opening lead is the ♠K.

Contract: 4 ♥

NORTH
♠ 9 6 3
♥ 6 5 4 2
♦ K Q J 3
♣ A 3

WEST
♠ K Q J 7 5
♥ –
♦ 10 5 4
♣ Q J 8 6 4

EAST
♠ A 10 4
♥ 10 9 8 7
♦ 8 7
♣ K 10 9 2

SOUTH
♠ 8 2
♥ A K Q J 3
♦ A 9 6 2
♣ 7 5

You can afford three losers and have two spade losers and one club loser. When you organise your plan, you want to play the cards in an order that does not put you in a position to create an extra loser. Look at what would happen if you did not draw the trumps. If you were to play diamonds, for example, the third round could be trumped by East. That is a loser you didn't count on.

You might think that using two of your trumps to draw out one of the opponents' trumps is not a good bargain. The alternative, however, is to let East enjoy a winner with one of his hearts. By drawing all his trumps, you prevent this.

Let's look at another example. This time you are in a partgame of 3 ♥. The lead is the ♣K.

Contract: 3 ♥

NORTH
♠ 10 5 2
♥ J 7 4 3
♦ A 10 8
♣ A 6 4

WEST
♠ J 7 6 3
♥ A K 2
♦ 9 2
♣ K Q 10 9

EAST
♠ Q 9 8 4
♥ 5
♦ J 6 5 4 3
♣ J 7 5

SOUTH
♠ A K
♥ Q 10 9 8 6
♦ K Q 7
♣ 8 3 2

This time you can afford four losers and so you aren't too concerned when the opponents drive out your ♣A, leaving you with two club losers. You are also missing the ♥A and the ♥K. You have no losers in either spades or diamonds so you should be able to make the contract. When you organise your plan, don't create an extra loser for yourself. Where could an extra loser be created? Look at the diamonds. If you try to take three rounds of diamonds before drawing trumps, West will score not only the ♥A and ♥K but the ♥2 as well. To avoid this, draw the trumps, even though you have to give up the lead twice to do this.

You don't mind giving West the trump tricks he has coming to him, the ♥A and ♥K, but you want to avoid an unnecessary loser in the trump suit. After winning the ♣A, play a heart. West will win the trick and the defenders can take their club tricks. They might then lead a diamond, which you will win. Lead another heart and again give West the lead. Now what can West do? Whatever he leads, you can win the tricks and draw his remaining trump. Now, you can take your diamond winners in comfort.

It might seem as if the only time you draw trumps is when you have the number of losers you can afford. So as not to leave that impression, let's look at one more hand where drawing trumps is a priority. You are in a partgame of 3 ♠ with the opening lead of the ♥Q.

Contract: 3 ♠

NORTH
♠ 10 8 6 3
♥ K 8
♦ A 4 2
♣ J 8 7 6

WEST
♠ 2
♥ Q J 10 7 4 2
♦ 10 8 3
♣ K Q 9

EAST
♠ J 7 5
♥ 9 5
♦ K Q J 5
♣ A 10 3 2

SOUTH
♠ A K Q 9 4
♥ A 6 3
♦ 9 7 6
♣ 5 4

You can afford four losers in your 3 ♠ contract. You have no spade losers, one heart loser, two diamond losers and two club losers. You need to get rid of one loser. Look for unevenly divided suits between your hand and the dummy to see if there is either the opportunity to trump a loser in the dummy or to get rid of a loser on one of the dummy's winners. When you look at the two hands for opportunities to get rid of losers, you see that there are more hearts in your hand than in the dummy and that there is an opportunity to trump a loser in the dummy. Unlike the first two examples, where you had the number of losers you could afford, this time you have to trump a loser in the dummy.

Does it matter whether you draw trumps first or trump a heart in the dummy first? Look at all four hands. If you try to trump a heart before getting rid of the trumps in the opponents' hands, East will be able to *overtrump* anything you can contribute in the dummy with his ♠J. You only need one trump to get rid of your heart loser. You do not have to give up the lead to draw trumps. Therefore, the best plan is to draw the trump and then get rid of your loser.

You cannot conclude that it is always the best idea to draw trumps before you go about trumping losers in the dummy. Each hand is different and you have to look at it in the context of your plan. As we have seen in previous chapters, on many hands where you are going to trump a loser in the dummy, you cannot afford to draw the trump. How can you know when playing trumps is right? Make your plan and use it to look ahead a few tricks. In the hand we just looked at, you knew you needed only one trump left in the dummy to take care of the heart loser in your hand, and you had four trumps. You could also see that drawing trumps would not give up the lead. You still had control of the hand. In this situation you had nothing to lose by drawing trumps before trumping your loser. The opponents could not get the lead and interrupt your plan.

Delaying drawing trumps

Let's look at two situations where you should delay drawing trumps. Remember, the reason you count losers when you are in a trump contract is that you have the opportunity, because of the power of the trumps, to get rid of those losers. You can either trump them in the dummy or you can throw away losers from your hand on the extra strength in the dummy. Both ways of getting rid of losers are closely connected to the trump suit.

First, if you are going to trump losers in the dummy, you have to make sure you have enough trumps in the dummy to do the job. In the last hand, we could comfortably draw trumps and still have a trump in dummy to take care of our loser. But that is not always, or normally, the case. More often, you have to guard your trumps carefully.

There is another important aspect of managing your trumps so that you have enough in the dummy to take care of the declarer's losers, and that is to remember that you have opponents. You are not the only player at the table who can draw trumps. You have first to decide how many trumps in the dummy you are going to need to take care of the losers in your hand. Then you have to consider how many times you have to give up the lead to the opponents before you are in a position to trump your losers. Before you go about drawing even a single round of trumps, consider what will happen if your opponents draw them for you. Let's look at a hand. You are in a contract of 2 ♦ and the opening lead is the ♣3.

Contract: 2 ♦

NORTH
♠ Q 8 3 2
♥ 7 4
♦ Q J 7
♣ 7 6 5 4

WEST
♠ J 9 7
♥ A J 6 3
♦ 6 4
♣ K J 8 3

EAST
♠ K 10 6 5
♥ K Q 8 2
♦ 5 3 2
♣ Q 9

SOUTH
♠ A 4
♥ 10 9 5
♦ A K 10 9 8
♣ A 10 2

You can afford five losers but it looks as if you have six: one spade, three hearts and two clubs. You have to get rid of one loser. What are the possibilities? You can't get rid of a spade loser since there are fewer cards in your hand than in the dummy and there is no extra strength in the suit in the dummy. The heart suit, if you look closely, has the right pattern to trump a loser in the dummy. You have three hearts in your hand and only two in the dummy. You need only one trump to take care of your heart loser and so you have to manage your trumps so that there is one left in the dummy.

The next observation to make is that you have to give the opponents the lead twice before you are in a position to trump your loser in the dummy. That means that the opponents could draw your trumps twice, leaving you with only one in the dummy. That you can afford. But, if you also draw a round of trumps, then you will be left with no diamonds to trump your losing heart trick and will be left with your original six losers. One occasion to avoid drawing trumps, then, is when you need to keep your trumps in the dummy to take care of a loser or losers in your hand.

The second way of getting rid of an extra loser is to throw it on one of the dummy's strong side suits. Should you draw the trumps before you do this? After all, you are not really counting on the dummy's trumps this time.

One consideration here is whether drawing the trumps would give up the lead. When you have to get rid of a loser, you may have to do it quickly, before you give the opponents the lead, because once they get in they might be able to take enough tricks to defeat the contract.

This is best seen by looking at a complete hand. The contract is 4 ♥ and the opening lead is the ♦Q.

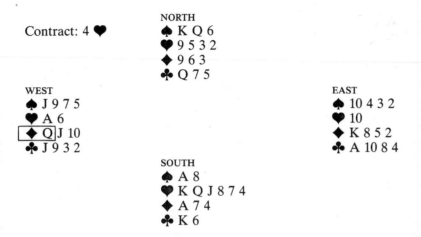

Contract: 4 ♥

NORTH
♠ K Q 6
♥ 9 5 3 2
♦ 9 6 3
♣ Q 7 5

WEST
♠ J 9 7 5
♥ A 6
♦ Q J 10
♣ J 9 3 2

EAST
♠ 10 4 3 2
♥ 10
♦ K 8 5 2
♣ A 10 8 4

SOUTH
♠ A 8
♥ K Q J 8 7 4
♦ A 7 4
♣ K 6

You can afford three losers. You have no spade losers, one heart loser, two diamond losers and one club loser, one too many. You need to get rid of one of your losers. Is there the opportunity to do this? Look for your unevenly divided side suits. There are more spades in the dummy than there are in your hand so this suit offers a good opportunity to get rid of a loser from your hand. A closer look shows that it is an excellent opportunity, since you have the first three tricks in the suit.

Are you going to draw the trumps before you try to get rid of your loser on the spade suit? Look ahead. What would happen if you started to draw the trumps? The opponents could take a trick with the ♥A. Now what would you expect them to do? They would take their two diamond winners and would probably be able to figure out to take the ♣A. You would have lost four tricks and would be defeated in your contract of 4 ♥.

You cannot give up the lead to the opponents before you get rid of a loser. So, suppose that instead of drawing trumps after you win the first trick with the ♦A, you play the spades and throw a diamond loser on the third round. Then you draw the trumps. Again, the opponents get the lead and try to take two diamond tricks. However, since you threw a diamond away, you can trump on the third round. You are successful in holding yourself to only three losers, enough to make the contract.

Summary

It is generally a good idea to draw the opponents' trumps as quickly as possible to prevent the opponents from playing a trump on one of your winners. Draw trumps in the following situations:

- When you have the winners you can afford — even if you have to give up the lead a couple of times in the process
- When you don't have enough tricks but you don't have to give up the lead, and don't need all your trumps to trump losers in the dummy

Delay drawing trumps in two situations:

- When you are going to need trumps in the dummy to take care of one or more losers in your hand, and you will not have enough left if you, or the opponents, draw trumps.
- When you would have to give up the lead to the opponents by drawing trumps and they can then take enough tricks to defeat your contract

Over Zia's shoulder

Hand 1 Dealer: East

DUMMY
♠ A Q
♥ K 2
♦ A K 7 6 4
♣ A K 4 3

OPENING LEAD:
♥ Q

DECLARER (ZIA)
♠ K J 9 8 7 4 2
♥ A 3
♦ 5 2
♣ 10 9

NORTH	EAST	SOUTH	WEST
		(Zia)	
	Pass	3 ♠	Pass
4 NT	Pass	5 ♦	Pass
7 ♠	Pass	Pass	Pass

Our first hand in this chapter is a grand slam. It seems easy enough, doesn't it? This hand will be fun to play together.

Solution to Hand 1:

Contract: 7 ♠

NORTH
♠ A Q
♥ K 2
♦ A K 7 6 4
♣ A K 4 3

WEST
♠ 10 6 5 3
♥ [Q] J 9 8 5
♦ J 9
♣ 8 6

EAST
♠ –
♥ 10 7 6 4
♦ Q 10 8 3
♣ Q J 7 5 2

SOUTH
♠ K J 9 8 7 4 2
♥ A 3
♦ 5 2
♣ 10 9

S   We can afford no losers.

T   We have no losers in spades, hearts, diamonds or clubs. That's good news.

O   Where could extra losers come from? Well, there is a possibility that if we don't draw the opponents' trump cards we could have an unexpected loser. This hand seems straightforward enough. There is one careless mistake we could make. Suppose we take the first heart trick with the ♥A in our hand. Does it really matter where we win the first heart? Let's follow through. We have to draw four rounds of trumps before the opponents' spades are exhausted because they are unfortunately divided 4–0. This should be no problem since we have the four top honours. So we are in our hand. We play the trumps and get stuck in the dummy. We can't afford to overtake the ♠Q with the ♠K or we would establish West's ♠10 as a trick. We have to find another way to get back to our hand to draw the trump. How can we get back to our hand? We could trump either a club or a diamond but would have to trump high with the king or jack or West could overtrump. Once we make the mistake of putting the ♥A on the first trick we can no longer make the contract.

P   Instead, we have to play the ♥K on the first trick. Now we play the two top trump from the dummy and come over to our hand with the ♥A and draw the rest of West's trumps. Now, we can enjoy the winners in the other suits. On this hand it was necessary to draw the trump in order to avoid an extra loser in the trump suit. To do this we had to be able to get to our long trumps and had to keep the high card with our long suit.

Hand 2 Dealer: South

                    DUMMY
                    ♠ 4 3
                    ♥ K 4 3
                    ♦ Q 10 2
                    ♣ J 10 8 7 2

OPENING LEAD:
♥ Q

                    DECLARER (ZIA)
                    ♠ 10 9 8 7 6 2
                    ♥ A 8
                    ♦ K J 3
                    ♣ K Q

NORTH	EAST	SOUTH	WEST
		(Zia)	
		1 ♠	Pass
1 NT	Pass	2 ♠	Pass
Pass	Pass		

When you first look at this hand there seems to be too much
to do. Where do we start?

Solution to Hand 2:

Contract: 2 ♠

NORTH
- ♠ 4 3
- ♥ K 4 3
- ♦ Q 10 2
- ♣ J 10 8 7 2

WEST
- ♠ A K 5
- ♥ Q J 10
- ♦ 9 8 7 6 4
- ♣ 9 5

EAST
- ♠ Q J
- ♥ 9 7 6 5 2
- ♦ A 5
- ♣ A 6 4 3

SOUTH
- ♠ 10 9 8 7 6 2
- ♥ A 8
- ♦ K J 3
- ♣ K Q

S   We can afford five losers.

T   Our loser count tells us that we have at least three spade losers — assuming they are divided 3–2 — one diamond loser and one club loser.

O   We can afford five losers. Are there any dangers in the hand? Yes. If we don't start by getting the opponents' trumps out of the way we are liable to find that they use their high trumps separately. We have enough length in the trumps not to worry. There is nothing to ruff in the dummy so we have no reason to delay drawing the trumps, even if it means giving them the lead three times.

P   So, we win the first heart trick and immediately lead a trump. When we next get the lead, we lead another trump. Once all their trumps are gone, we have no more worries. If we didn't decide on this plan, they will probably get an extra trick in the trump suit, which they don't deserve.

Hand 3 Dealer: South

DUMMY
♠ 8 4 2
♥ A Q 9 7
♦ 9 8 7
♣ Q J 3

OPENING LEAD:
♦ Q

DECLARER (ZIA)
♠ K Q J 10 9 7
♥ K 2
♦ A 6 5
♣ K 4

NORTH	EAST	SOUTH (Zia)	WEST
		1 ♠	Pass
1 NT	Pass	3 ♠	Pass
4 ♠	Pass	Pass	Pass

It is annoying, but West has again found the best lead. On any other lead we would be waltzing. Well, never say die.

Solution to Hand 3:

Contract: 4 ♠

NORTH
♠ 8 4 2
♥ A Q 9 7
♦ 9 8 7
♣ Q J 3

WEST
♠ 6 5
♥ 10 5 4 3
♦ Q J 2
♣ A 7 6 5

EAST
♠ A 3
♥ J 8 6
♦ K 10 4 3
♣ 10 9 8 2

SOUTH
♠ K Q J 10 9 7
♥ K 2
♦ A 6 5
♣ K 4

S   We can afford three losers.

T   It looks as if there is a spade loser, two diamond losers and a club loser. We have to get rid of one.

O   Normally, in a suit contract, we like to go after the trumps as soon as possible. That is a pretty useful guideline, but only when there is no more urgent job. Here, if we win the diamond lead and start our trumps, the nasty opponents — opponents are nearly always nasty! — might take two diamond tricks and the ♠A and the ♣A. That won't do! We'll have to delay drawing trumps until we first discard one of our losing diamonds on the ♥Q.

P   After winning the ♦A, we'll start playing the hearts with the ♥K, high card from the short side. After a diamond loser has been discarded on the extra heart winner in the dummy, we can go about drawing the trumps.

Chapter 9

More About High Cards

It is never too early or too late to learn to play bridge.

When playing a hand, you often look to the four honours in each suit — the ace, king, queen and jack — to take tricks. If, however, you see these cards only in the light of their ability to take a single trick, you are underestimating their importance. Let's first consider the ace. Certainly it is usually good for taking a trick. But did you know that it has the power to prevent the opponents from taking their winners? Or to enable you, the declarer, to be in the right place at the right time in order to take winners of less potency? The ace, and your other high cards, are valuable members of your team of high cards.

Using high cards to prevent the opponents from taking winners

A high card in a suit only wins a trick if you manage to play it. We have all had the sad experience of looking at winners in our hand and knowing that we are never going to enjoy them. Taking winners consists not only of developing the winners in the first place but also being in the right place at the right time. Consider this layout of the diamond suit. You are in a no-trump contract and West leads the ♦K.

```
                        DUMMY
                        ♦ 4 3 2

WEST                                                    EAST
♦ K Q J 10 9 8                                          ♦ 7 6
                        DECLARER
                        ♦ A 5
```

It looks as if you have only one trick in the suit, which you can win with the ♦A. The opponents, on the other hand, have established five winners after your ♦A is played. At first glance, there may seem to be nothing you can do about the situation. But remember, winners are only good if you have a way to get to them. It is true that your ace has the power to take only one trick. Another way of looking at the situation, however, is to consider not only the trick-taking power of the card but the way it can control a suit. Played at the right time, it may prevent the opponents from taking all five of their diamond tricks. Timing is everything.

Suppose you play your ♦A on the ♦K. Unless you can immediately take enough tricks to make your contract, you will have to give the lead to the opponents while you are developing the winners you need. If West gets the lead, he will take his diamond winners. If East gets the lead, he will be able to lead his remaining small diamond to West's promoted winners. Either way, the opponents take five diamond tricks. What can you do to prevent this?

Suppose you don't play your ♦A until the second trick. The defenders will have collected one diamond trick. What has changed? You still may have to give up the lead to the opponents. This time, however, if it is East who gets the lead, he will have no diamonds left to lead back to West's winners. Of course, West may have an entry in another suit, or it may be West that gets the lead when you are developing the winners you need. Too bad. At least you gave yourself the best chance. By holding up your ace until the second round, you may hold the opponents to only one trick in the diamond suit.

Let's look at this idea in a complete hand. You are in 3 NT and the opening lead is the ♦K.

Contract: 3 NT

NORTH
♠ Q 8 7
♥ 8 5 3
♦ 8 7
♣ K 9 6 5 2

WEST
♠ 10 9 3 2
♥ 7 4
♦ K Q J 10 9
♣ Q 8

EAST
♠ 6 4
♥ A 10 9 6
♦ 4 3 2
♣ J 10 4 3

SOUTH
♠ A K J 5
♥ K Q J 2
♦ A 6 5
♣ A 7

You need to take nine tricks to make your contract of 3 NT. Count your winners: four spades, one diamond and two clubs, a total of seven. Two more winners need to be developed and the heart suit offers a good opportunity to promote the winners you need. Organise your plan. If you plan to take the ♦A on the first trick and try to develop your heart winners, whichever defender wins the ♥A will be able to lead a diamond and the defenders can take all their diamond winners. On the actual hand, West has four promoted winners and the defenders defeat your contract.

We need to organise a plan with more chance of success. This time, let West win the first two diamond tricks and take the third round of diamonds with the ♦A. After three rounds of diamonds have been played you have lost only two tricks. Now, try to promote your heart winners. East takes the trick with the ♥A, you can't prevent that. However, on the actual hand, East has no diamonds left to get back into West's hand and has to lead another suit. Whether East chooses spades, hearts or clubs, you are ready to take your nine tricks.

Are we just lucky that East has the ♥A and no diamonds left? Not really. The opponents have eight cards in the diamond suit and you would expect them to be divided 5–3. If East had a diamond left to lead back when he won the ♥A, they would have originally been divided 4–4 and the opponents would only end up with three diamond tricks and one heart trick. You would still make the contract. At any rate, if West holds the ♥A along with a five-card diamond suit, there is nothing you can do to make your contract. You gave it the best chance.

114

When you choose to play low on a trick when you could win it, it is called a *holdup play*. The ace is not the only card you can use when making a holdup play. After the ace has been played, the king, the next highest card, takes over the ace's position and its importance. In the previous example, we saw that, by holding up the ace, you can prevent the defenders from getting to their promoted winners. When the ace has been played, holding up the king can have the same effect. Consider this layout. You are in 3 NT and West leads a small diamond, the ♦7:

DUMMY
♦ 4 3

WEST
♦ Q 10 8 7 6

EAST
♦ A J 5

DECLARER
♦ K 9 2

You play a small card from the dummy, East takes the first trick with the ♦A, and leads another diamond. After the ♦A has been played, your ♦K is the highest outstanding card in the suit. If you take it on the second round, diamonds will have been played twice, with one trick won by the defenders and one trick by you. The layout of the suit would now be the following:

DUMMY
♦ –

WEST
♦ Q 10 8

EAST
♦ 5

DECLARER
♦ 9

You have the lead and, unless you are taking the next eight tricks, enough to make your contract, you will have to give the lead to the opponents while developing the extra winners you need. Whether East or West gets the lead, the defenders are ready to take three diamond tricks.

Suppose, on the second round of the suit, you hold up your ♦ K. East can play the suit again and, on the third round, you take ♦ K. Now diamonds have been played three times. You have taken one trick with the ♦ K and the opponents have taken two tricks. The layout of the suit is now:

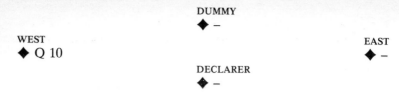

DUMMY
♦ —

WEST
♦ Q 10

EAST
♦ —

DECLARER
♦ —

Although West has two established winners, they are of no value if East gets the lead. He has to lead another suit and with luck, you are then in a position to take enough tricks to make your contract. This isn't a guaranteed method of making your contract, but it does give you a 50 per cent chance.

Notice the difference between the above situation and this layout:

DUMMY
♦ 4 3

WEST
♦ A J 8 7 6

EAST
♦ Q 10 9

DECLARER
♦ K 5 2

If West leads a small diamond and East puts on the ♦Q, your ♦K does not have the power of the ace because the ♦A has not been played. This is not the time to hold up your king. You will have to take it — to avoid the possibility of losing the first five diamond tricks — and hope you can develop the tricks you need without giving up the lead to the opponents.

Using high cards as entries

High cards can provide a means of transport from one side of the table to another. Why is this important? Not only do you need entries to get to your promoted or established winners, you also need them to be able to try finesses. In order to lead towards the card you hope will take a trick, you have to be in the hand opposite the high card — and that requires an entry. You also need to be on the right side of the table to trump losers in the dummy or to throw away a loser in the declarer's hand on the dummy's extra strength.

High cards as entries to small cards in long suits

Long suits provide an excellent opportunity to develop the extra tricks to make your contract. When a small card is part of a long suit, it can be developed into a winner. Usually, your long suits have one or two honour cards and these have to be carefully handled, being played at the right time in order to take best advantage of them. Let's first consider a suit which has length in the dummy but no outside card to get to any established winners. That means that the dummy's high card in the suit has to be carefully handled.

DUMMY

♣ A 5 4 3 2

WEST   EAST

♣ K Q 9   ♣ J 10

DECLARER

♣ 8 7 6

The ♣A will take one trick in the club suit. You want to be more ambitious than expecting only one trick from this suit, however. You are hoping the five cards that the opponents have are distributed as in the layout, 3–2. You can get one trick with the ♣A, lose two tricks to the opponents and thereby establish the two remaining clubs in the dummy as winners — provided you can get to them. The ♣A provides not only a trick, but also your means of transport to the established winners. If you play the ♣A on the first or second trick, you have no way of getting the winners. On the other hand, if you lose two tricks and then take your ♣A on the third round, you are not only winning the trick you expected with the ♣A, but you have taken it at the right time, after your small cards are established. In total, you take three tricks in the suit.

High cards as entries to your promoted winners

When you are promoting winners in one suit, you often need an entry in another suit to get to the promoted winners. Sometimes, when you have both an ace and a king in a side suit, you might think it doesn't matter the order in which you play these high cards. Nothing could be further from the truth. The high cards are so important that the order is usually very important. In order to emphasise this point, let's consider an entire hand. You are in a contract of 3 NT and West leads the ♦Q. Since you have both the ◆A and the ◆K, you have a choice of which you play on the first trick. Which honour would you use to take the first trick?

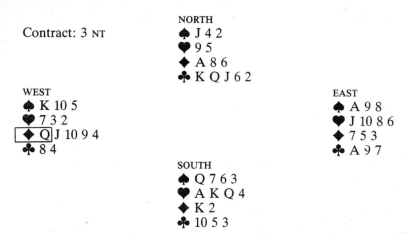

Contract: 3 NT

NORTH
♠ J 4 2
♥ 9 5
◆ A 8 6
♣ K Q J 6 2

WEST
♠ K 10 5
♥ 7 3 2
◆ Q J 10 9 4
♣ 8 4

EAST
♠ A 9 8
♥ J 10 8 6
◆ 7 5 3
♣ A 9 7

SOUTH
♠ Q 7 6 3
♥ A K Q 4
◆ K 2
♣ 10 5 3

You need nine tricks to make the contract. You have three sure heart tricks, and two diamonds, a total of five tricks. Four more need to be developed and the club suit offers excellent potential. After the ♣A is driven out, you will have promoted the four tricks you need to make your contract. East will probably make things as difficult as possible by holding up the ♣A until the third round. You will have taken two tricks in the suit, and will have lost one. Your two clubs in the dummy are promoted as winners. All you have to do is get to them. Which diamond did you play on the first trick? Let's hope you played the ◆K from your hand, leaving the ◆A in the dummy as an entry to your promoted clubs. You can see on this hand that the diamonds not only took two tricks but provided the potential for two extra tricks in another suit. The high cards are a very important part of the team.

Using your high cards to take a finesse
There is another reason for entries. Take a look at this layout:

DUMMY
♠ 8 7

DECLARER
♠ A Q

The ♠A and ♠Q will take only one trick if you lead them

from your hand. On the other hand, if you lead a low spade from the dummy towards the ace-queen combination, there is the potential for two tricks in the suit: one with the ♠A and one with the ♠Q. It isn't a 100 per cent chance, but it is a 50 per cent chance and that is worth trying if that is the only way of getting the extra trick you need. In order to take a trick with the ♠Q you have to start from the dummy. You therefore need an entry to the dummy.

The following hand shows how carefully your entries have to be used. The contract is 4 ♥ and the opening lead is the ♦2:

Contract: 4 ♥

```
                    NORTH
                    ♠ 6 4 2
                    ♥ A Q 10
                    ♦ 9 6 3
                    ♣ Q J 4 2
WEST                                        EAST
♠ 8 3                                       ♠ K 9 7 5
♥ 6 3 2                                     ♥ 8 4
♦ Q 10 7 [2]                                ♦ K J 8 5
♣ A 8 6 3                                   ♣ K 10 9
                    SOUTH
                    ♠ A Q J 10
                    ♥ K J 9 7 5
                    ♦ A 4
                    ♣ 7 5
```

You can afford only three losers and it looks as though you will have to lose a diamond trick and two club tricks. So you cannot afford to lose a spade trick, even though you are missing the ♠K. You will have to hope that East has the ♠K and you can take repeated finesses through him to avoid losing a spade trick. What are you going to use for entries to the dummy? Only the trump suit will provide the entries you need. Since you may have to repeat the finesse three times, you will have carefully to combine drawing trumps with leading spades from the dummy at every opportunity.

After winning the first diamond trick, play a heart to one of the dummy's high cards and lead a small spade towards your hand. Assuming East follows with a small spade, finesse the ♠10 (or ♠J or ♠Q). When this wins, cross back to the dummy with another heart and lead another low spade, repeating the finesse. As you cross to the dummy for a third time, you draw the last

119

trump and end up in the right place to lead your final small spade from the dummy and take one more finesse. Only by careful use of each of the dummy's high hearts can you make the contract.

Using high cards as entries for getting rid of losers

Let's see how important our high cards are in helping to be in the right hand when trumping losers in the dummy. The contract is 6 ♠ and the lead is the ♠3:

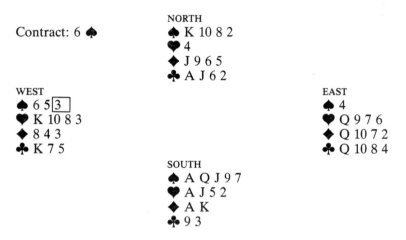

Contract: 6 ♠

NORTH
♠ K 10 8 2
♥ 4
♦ J 9 6 5
♣ A J 6 2

WEST
♠ 6 5 3
♥ K 10 8 3
♦ 8 4 3
♣ K 7 5

EAST
♠ 4
♥ Q 9 7 6
♦ Q 10 7 2
♣ Q 10 8 4

SOUTH
♠ A Q J 9 7
♥ A J 5 2
♦ A K
♣ 9 3

To make your slam, you can only afford one loser. There are three heart losers and a club loser to worry about and, since there is not much you can do about the club loser, you plan to trump the heart losers in the dummy. West's trump lead, removing one of the dummy's trumps, has not helped your cause. You cannot afford to use your trumps as entries or let the opponents in to lead another trump, as that would leave you with too few trumps in the dummy. Instead, win the trump lead and immediately play the ♥A and trump a heart in the dummy. Use the ♦A and trump your last heart in the dummy. The only loser you are left with is a club and you end up making the contract.

Finally, let's look at a hand where you need to discard a loser:

Contract: 4 ♣

NORTH
♠ 10 8 2
♥ K 7 5
♦ K Q 8 4
♣ A 9 4

WEST
♠ J 9 3
♥ J 8 6 3
♦ 10 6
♣ Q J 10 2

EAST
♠ 6 4
♥ 10 9 4 2
♦ A J 9 3
♣ K 8 5

SOUTH
♠ A K Q 7 5
♥ A Q
♦ 7 5 2
♣ 7 6 3

In 4 ♠, you can afford three losers. Provided the missing trumps are divided 3–2, you will not have to lose a spade trick, but you will have two losers in diamonds and in clubs. If West has the ♦A, you can lead twice towards the dummy's ♦K and ♦Q to lose only one diamond trick. But, if the ♦A is with East, you will have to find another way to take care of your second diamond loser. The heart suit provides an opportunity to discard one of your losers, but you will have to plan the play carefully since the club lead has driven out the dummy's only quick entry. Win the ♣A, draw trumps, and then play the ♥A and ♥Q. Now you can lead a diamond to create an entry to the dummy's ♥K. Once you get to the dummy with the ♦K or ♦Q, discard your remaining diamond loser on the ♥K.

Your high cards are important not only for the tricks they can take but for the influence they have in enabling you to take the tricks you have worked to develop and to prevent the opponents from taking the tricks they have developed.

Summary

The high cards in the deck are a good source for taking a trick. They have other powers. By using the holdup play, you can prevent the opponents from taking good tricks because your holdup has prevented them from getting to their winners. When you have the tricks you need, you have to get to them and the high cards provide a means of transport to get from one side of the table to another. This is important not only in taking your high cards but in developing the extra tricks you need through promotion, length in a suit and the finesse which can be used in either no-trump or suit contract. The high cards are also important entries when you are getting rid of your losers by either trumping in the dummy or throwing away losers on the dummy's extra strength.

Over Zia's shoulder

Hand 1 Dealer: North

DUMMY
♠ K Q 8 7
♥ K Q 6 2
♦ A Q
♣ 7 4 3

OPENING LEAD:
♦ 4

DECLARER (ZIA)
♠ A J 6 5 3
♥ A J 9
♦ J 6
♣ Q 8 2

NORTH	EAST	SOUTH (Zia)	WEST
1 ♥	Pass	1 ♠	Pass
3 ♣	Pass	4 ♥	Pass
4 ♠	Pass		

What should we play on the first diamond trick? It is always tempting to take a finesse when we have been given the opportunity to make use of our high cards in this fashion. However, our high cards can be useful in other ways as well. Let's go through the plan before making our decision.

122

Solution to Hand 1:

Contract: 4 ♠

NORTH
♠ K Q 8 7
♥ K Q 6 2
♦ A Q
♣ 7 4 3

WEST
♠ 10
♥ 8 5 4 3
♦ 10 8 7 4 3
♣ K 6 5

EAST
♠ 9 4 2
♥ 10 7
♦ K 9 5 2
♣ A J 10 9

SOUTH
♠ A J 6 5 3
♥ A J 9
♦ J 6
♣ Q 8 2

S   We can afford only three losers in our contract of 4 ♠.

T   We have a diamond loser and three club losers.

O   We could try the diamond finesse, getting rid of our diamond loser if West holds the ♦K. Is there anything else? We have an extra heart winner in the dummy and we could use it to discard one of our club losers. Is there any danger in trying the finesse first and, if it does not work, later discarding one of our club losers? There certainly is! If the finesse loses, East will probably not be kind enough to give us the opportunity to discard a club loser. He will switch to clubs and the opponents will take their three club winners, defeating the contract.

P   One of the extra powers of an ace is its ability to give us control of a suit by taking a trick at the right time. On this hand, we must take the ♦A right away, rather than yielding to the temptation of the finesse — which, as the cards lie, doesn't work out. We then draw the opponents' trumps and play our heart suit, eventually discarding one of our losers. Playing this way, we guarantee success, no matter which defender holds the ♦K.

Hand 2 Dealer: East

DUMMY
- ♠ Q J 7
- ♥ 9 5
- ♦ K 10 8 7 5
- ♣ A K 8

OPENING LEAD:
♥ 4

DECLARER (ZIA)
- ♠ A 10 9 2
- ♥ A 6 3
- ♦ Q J 6
- ♣ Q J 4

NORTH	EAST	SOUTH (Zia)	WEST
	Pass	1 NT	Pass
3 NT	Pass	Pass	Pass

It looks as though we have a choice of taking a spade finesse or driving out the ♦A to develop the extra tricks we need. Are there any other considerations?

Solution to Hand 2:

Contract: 3 NT

NORTH
- ♠ Q J 7
- ♥ 9 5
- ♦ K 10 8 7 5
- ♣ A K 8

WEST
- ♠ K 8
- ♥ Q 10 8 4 2
- ♦ 9 3
- ♣ 10 6 3 2

EAST
- ♠ 6 5 4 3
- ♥ K J 7
- ♦ A 4 2
- ♣ 9 7 5

SOUTH
- ♠ A 10 9 2
- ♥ A 6 3
- ♦ Q J 6
- ♣ Q J 4

S   We need to come up with nine tricks to make this contract.

T   We have one sure spade trick, one heart trick and three club tricks, for a total of five.

O   We need four more tricks. We could try leading the ♠Q or ♠J from the dummy, hoping to trap the ♠K in the East hand. That would give us three more tricks. Even if the finesse loses, we will have promoted two extra winners. The diamond suit, however, offers the opportunity to develop all four extra tricks, once the ♦A has been driven out. Is there anything else to worry about? West has attacked our weakness. Once our ♥A is gone, the opponents may be able to take enough heart tricks to defeat the contract when they get the lead with the ♦A. We had better make use of the holdup play.

P   We let the opponents win the first heart trick, and the second heart trick. Only when they lead the third round of hearts do we win the trick with our ♥A. Now we lead the ♦Q and continue leading high diamonds until the ♦A is driven out. Luckily for us, it is East who holds the ♦A and, thanks to our holdup play, he has no hearts left to lead. If he leads a spade, we quickly take the ♠A and run for home with our nine tricks. There is no point in risking the spade finesse. If it loses, we would let West — the opponent with the established heart winners — get the lead. We'll take our sure profit. On the

125

actual layout, we would be defeated if we played the hand any other way.

Hand 3 Dealer: West

DUMMY
- ♠ 8 4 2
- ♥ K 9 5
- ♦ 7 6 3
- ♣ J 7 5 2

OPENING LEAD:
♠ J

DECLARER (ZIA)
- ♠ A Q 7
- ♥ 8 6 4 2
- ♦ A K 9
- ♣ A K Q

NORTH	EAST	SOUTH	WEST
		(Zia)	
			Pass
Pass	Pass	2 NT	Pass
3 NT	Pass	Pass	Pass

It looks as though we may have some difficulty coming to nine tricks with these cards. West's opening lead has simplified things a little, since we are now assured of getting two spade tricks, whichever player has the ♠K. What's our plan?

127

Solution to Hand 3:

Contract: 3 NT

NORTH
- ♠ 8 4 2
- ♥ K 9 5
- ♦ 7 6 3
- ♣ J 7 5 2

WEST
- ♠ J 10 9 5 3
- ♥ A Q
- ♦ J 5 4
- ♣ 9 4 3

EAST
- ♠ K 6
- ♥ J 10 7 3
- ♦ Q 10 8 2
- ♣ 10 8 6

SOUTH
- ♠ A Q 7
- ♥ 8 6 4 2
- ♦ A K 9
- ♣ A K Q

S   We need to find nine winners.

T   We have two sure spade tricks, the ♠A and ♠Q, since West has led a spade. We also have two sure diamond tricks and four sure club tricks. That's eight tricks to start with.

O   The best place for a ninth trick is the heart suit. If West has the ♥A, we can get a trick by leading towards the dummy's ♥K. Are there any other problems? We are counting on four club tricks but we have to get to the dummy in order to take our fourth club trick and the dummy has no sure entry. We will have to make the ♥K do double work. Not only will it have to provide our ninth trick but it will also have to be our entry to the dummy. That means we will have to be careful about the order in which we play our cards.

P   After winning the first spade trick, we'll have to play the ♣A, ♣K and ♣Q. Now we lead a small heart towards the dummy and hope. When West turns out to have the ♥A, our problems are over. We will get to the dummy with the ♥K and, while we are there, we can take a trick with the ♣J. Careful play lands us nine tricks.

Chapter 10

The Plan's The Thing

No matter where you travel, there is a game of bridge and therefore new friends nearby.

We have come full circle. In the first chapter, we asked whether you should play the ace or the queen on the first trick of a hand. Before you could answer, you had to consider the question in the context of the whole hand. As you have seen throughout the book, on every hand, before you can decide whether to develop tricks by promotion, or length or through the finesse or, in fact, whether you need to develop tricks at all, you have to consult your plan. The plan's the thing.

Putting the plan into action

Let's see how the steps of our plan can help you with the following suit combination when West leads the king:

DUMMY
♥ 7 3

WEST
♥ K

DECLARER
♥ A 6 4

The suit itself looks simple enough since you only have one

trick to take, the ♥A. It may make a big difference, however, whether you win the ♥A on the first, second or third round of the suit. The only way you can decide when to win your ace is by first going through the steps of your plan.

For example, suppose you are in a contract of 3 NT and these are the combined hands:

DUMMY
♠ A J 5
♥ 7 3
♦ A Q 8 6
♣ 9 7 4 2

OPENING LEAD:
♥ K

DECLARER
♠ K Q 7 3
♥ A 6 4
♦ K J 5 2
♣ J 3

Let's use the letters S T O P. You stop to consider your goal, which is to take nine tricks. Then you tally your winners. You have four spade tricks, one heart trick and four diamond tricks — a total of nine, enough to make the contract. Organise your plan. You have enough tricks to make the contract so you need look no further. Put your plan into action by winning the first trick with the ♥A and then taking your spade and diamond winners.

Easy as pie. How did the plan help you? It stopped you from instinctively holding up with the ♥A, trying to make it difficult for the opponents to get their heart winners. Look at what might happen if you did not win the first trick. West might decide to switch to the club suit and it is quite likely that the opponents could take four or more tricks in that suit and defeat the contract.

Now, let's suppose we keep your heart suit and the contract the same — 3 NT — but make a few changes to the rest of the hand:

♠ 10 7 2
♥ 7 3
♦ K J 7 3
♣ A Q 6 2

OPENING LEAD:
♥ K

DECLARER
♠ A K 9 5
♥ A 6 4
♦ Q 10 5
♣ K 8 5

What does the plan tell you this time? Stop to consider your goal. Again, you need to take nine tricks. Tally your winners. You have two spade tricks, one heart trick and three club tricks for a total of six tricks. Organise your plan. You need three more tricks. The diamonds offer an excellent opportunity to establish the extra tricks through promotion. Is there any danger? Suppose that you play the ♥A on the first trick, as you did in the first example. What would happen next? When you drive out the ♦A, whichever opponent wins the trick will lead another heart and the opponents will take their established heart tricks. If West started with five or more hearts, your contract will go down to defeat. Is there anything you can do? This is a classic situation for the holdup play. Wait until the third round of hearts before taking your ♥A. Now, if East has the ♦A and the missing hearts are divided 5–3, East will have no heart left to lead and you will make the contract.

Only by going through the plan, can you determine that on this hand, the best play is to win the heart on the third round. Is there ever a time when you would want to win the ♥A on the second round? Consider the following hand. This time, you are in a contract of 4 ♠.

131

♠ A K 8
♥ 7 3
♦ 10 7 6 2
♣ A K Q 5

♥ K

DECLARER
♠ Q 7 5 3 2
♥ A 6 4
♦ Q 8
♣ 9 4 2

Since you are in a trump contract, you look at your goal from the point of view of losers. You can afford three losers. You will not have to lose a spade trick if the missing spades divide 3–2 because you can draw all the opponents' trumps with your ♠A, ♠K and ♠Q. However, you still have two heart losers and two diamond losers to worry about. In organising your plan, it looks as though the best approach is to try to trump your heart loser with the dummy's small trump. Does it matter when you win the ♥A?

In order to trump your heart loser, you are going to have to give up one trick to the opponents. Suppose you win the first heart trick and then lead another heart. The opponents can win and, seeing what you are planning to do, lead a trump. How can you reach your hand to trump your loser? You cannot win the trick with the ♠Q in your hand since you would now have to trump your loser with the dummy's ♠A or ♠K. You would then not be able to draw the opponents' trumps without losing a trick. If you win the spade trick in the dummy, you have no entry to your hand.

Instead, all you have to do is let the opponents win the first heart trick. If they now lead a spade, you can win in the dummy and lead the dummy's remaining small heart to your carefully preserved ♥A. Then you can trump your heart loser with the dummy's small spade and use your high spades to draw trumps.

In addition to telling you how to play a particular suit, your plan will help you determine which suit to play. Consider the following suit combinations:

1 DUMMY	**2** DUMMY	**3** DUMMY
♥ K Q	♦ A Q	♣ A K Q 5
DECLARER	DECLARER	DECLARER
♥ 4 3	♦ 4 3	♣ 4 3 2

Suppose you need to develop one extra trick. In the first combination, you have no sure tricks but you can always develop an extra trick by driving out the opponents' ♥A. In the second combination, you have one sure trick and might be able to develop a second trick by leading towards the dummy and finessing the ♦Q. Unlike the first layout, the chance of success here is only 50 per cent since it depends on which opponent holds the missing ♦K. In the third combination, you start with three sure tricks and you may develop a fourth trick through length. After playing the ♣A, ♣K and ♣Q, the dummy's ♣5 will be a trick if the opponents' clubs are divided exactly 3–3. The chances of this happening are less than 50 per cent since the odds favour the missing cards dividing 4–2 — and they may even be divided 5–1 or 6–0.

Does this mean that you would always prefer the first combination to the second, or the second to the third, when you have to develop an extra trick? Until you've gone through the steps of the plan, you cannot be sure. Take a look at the following hand, where you are in a contract of 3 NT:

DUMMY
♠ A 7
♥ 4 3 2
♦ 4 3
♣ A Q J 7 5 3

OPENING LEAD:
♠ 6

DECLARER
♠ 9 3
♥ K Q 5
♦ A Q 6 5
♣ K 9 4 2

Your objective is to take nine tricks and you have a spade trick, a diamond trick and six club tricks, for a total of eight. Only one more trick needs to be developed. Organise your plan. There are two options for developing a ninth trick. You can play hearts, driving out the ace and promoting a winner, or you can take the diamond finesse. On the surface, playing the heart suit appears to be the best option since you are sure to develop the extra trick you need, while the diamond finesse will only succeed half the time.

Before putting your plan into action, however, you need to consider what will happen when the opponents win a trick with their ♥A. They have led spades and even if you holdup your ♠A on the first round, they will lead spades again and drive it out. Unless one opponent started with seven spades — highly unlikely — both the opponents will have spades left when they get the lead with the ♥A. Even if the spades are divided as evenly as possible, 5–4, the opponents will be able to take four spade tricks to go along with the heart trick and defeat the contract. Playing the heart suit will almost certainly lead to defeat. On the other hand, if the diamond finesse is successful, you will not have to let the opponents regain the lead before you have taken nine tricks. Even though it is only a 50 per cent chance, it is better than no chance at all.

So, your plan tells you to play diamonds rather than hearts in the above hand. Now, consider this hand where you have climbed all the way to a contract of 7 NT:

DUMMY
♠ A Q 7
♥ A 7 4 3
♦ 4 3
♣ A K Q 5

OPENING LEAD:
♥ 10

DECLARER
♠ K J 9 3
♥ K Q J 5
♦ A Q
♣ 4 3 2

This time, you need all the tricks. You have four spade tricks, four heart tricks, a diamond trick and three club tricks. With twelve tricks off the top, you need to find one more. There are two choices. You can try the diamond finesse or hope that the missing clubs are divided 3–3. Again, at first glance, it would appear that the diamond finesse offers the better chance since the missing clubs will be divided 3–3 less than half the time. If you organise the play carefully, however, you can take advantage of both chances, rather than only one. There is no hurry. You can plan to take your spade and heart tricks and then play the ♣A, ♣K and ♣Q. If the missing clubs turn out to be divided 3–3, dummy's ♣5 has become your thirteenth trick and you do not need to take the diamond finesse. If the missing clubs are not divided 3–3, you can fall back on the diamond finesse as your second chance.

Your plan helps you organise the play of the hand to best combine your chances. It also points out that you must keep your eye on the club suit as you play the hand. You will need to watch the cards the opponents play to determine whether or not the ♣5 is your thirteenth trick. After all, even if one of the opponents held four clubs originally, he might discard one when you take your spade and heart tricks! Once you've made your plan, you know where to focus your effort during the play.

Summary

Before you make a decision on how to play a particular suit, or whether or not to play a suit, you need to consult your plan. You need to know how many tricks you need or how many losers you can afford, and what options you have. In organising your plan, choose the option that gives you the best chance of making the contract, trying to combine options whenever possible. Take a look at what may happen if you have to give up the lead to the opponents. Only then are you ready to put the plan into action and play your first card.

Over Zia's shoulder

Hand 1 Dealer: West

DUMMY
- ♠ A Q
- ♥ A 8 4
- ♦ K Q J 10 8
- ♣ Q 6 5

OPENING LEAD:
♠ 4

DECLARER (ZIA)
- ♠ J 7 6
- ♥ 6 5 2
- ♦ 9 4 3
- ♣ A K 7 4

NORTH	EAST	SOUTH (Zia)	WEST
			Pass
1 ♦	Pass	1 NT	Pass
3 NT	Pass	Pass	Pass

Here we are, ending our journey together, talking about whether to finesse or not. Let's make our plan. This looks easy enough, but I am always a bit suspicious when Audrey hasn't selected a tough hand for a while. Could this be it?

Solution to Hand 1:

Contract: 3 NT

NORTH
- ♠ A Q
- ♥ A 8 4
- ♦ K Q J 10 8
- ♣ Q 6 5

WEST
- ♠ 10 8 5 4 3 2
- ♥ 9 7 3
- ♦ 7 6
- ♣ J 9

EAST
- ♠ K 9
- ♥ K Q J 10
- ♦ A 5 2
- ♣ 10 8 3 2

SOUTH
- ♠ J 7 6
- ♥ 6 5 2
- ♦ 9 4 3
- ♣ A K 7 4

Well, we're not going to be so quick as to play the ♠Q without a little thought.

S   We have to take nine tricks.

T   We have one spade, one heart and three club tricks, a total of five.

O   There are three places where we might think about getting extra tricks. We might consider playing the ♠Q to gain an extra trick. If West has the ♠K, we gain a trick immediately. If East has the ♠K, our ♠J will be promoted to a winner. We can promote four winners in diamonds by driving out the ♦A. We also might get an extra trick from the club suit if the missing clubs are divided 3–3. Since the diamonds will provide all the tricks we need, this is the suit we want to focus on.

P   Since our plan tells us that we don't need an extra trick from the spade suit, we should win the ♠A and go about our business of developing the diamond suit. What would have happened if we took the spade finesse? East would win and lead back a heart, driving out our ♥A. The opponents would end up with five tricks: the ♠K, three heart tricks and the ♦A. Instead, we have to be quicker at promoting our diamonds while we have control. After we take the ♠A and play a diamond, East can take the ♦A and also the ♠K but must then give us back the lead since we still have the ♠J left. Timing is everything.

137

Hand 2 Dealer: East

DUMMY
- ♠ J 6 5 3
- ♥ K 8 7 5
- ♦ 9 6 3
- ♣ A 7

OPENING LEAD:
♣ Q

DECLARER (ZIA)
- ♠ A Q 10 9 8 7
- ♥ A Q
- ♦ 8 5 2
- ♣ K 8

NORTH	EAST	SOUTH (Zia)	WEST
	Pass	1 ♠	Pass
2 ♠	Pass	3 ♠	Pass
4 ♠	Pass	Pass	Pass

Contracts in the spade suit always remind me of a lion — a king of the jungle syndrome. But what dangers lurk in the forest? I wonder.

Solution to Hand 2:

Contract: 4 ♠

NORTH
♠ J 6 5 3
♥ K 8 7 5
♦ 9 6 3
♣ A 7

WEST
♠ K 2
♥ 10 6 4 2
♦ A J 10
♣ [Q] J 10 2

EAST
♠ 4
♥ J 9 3
♦ K Q 7 4
♣ 9 6 5 4 3

SOUTH
♠ A Q 10 9 8 7
♥ A Q
♦ 8 5 2
♣ K 8

S   We can afford to lose three tricks in our 4 ♠ contract.

T   We have one potential spade loser and three diamond losers, one too many.

O   It is tempting to take the first trick with the ♣A and try the spade finesse, trying to get rid of our extra loser that way. We should examine all the possibilities, however, before deciding on our plan. The dummy has an extra heart winner and we could use it to discard one of our diamond losers. This is a better alternative than taking the spade finesse right away. If it does not work — perhaps one of the opponents will trump our heart winner — we can fall back on the spade finesse later.

P   One more thought before we play to the first trick. We will need the ♣A as an entry to the dummy, so we should win the first trick with the ♣K in our hand. Then we play the ♥A and ♥Q. Now it is time for the ♣A so that we can get to the dummy to play the ♥K and discard a diamond loser. When this works successfully, we can turn our attention to the spade suit. We no longer mind that the finesse loses. Lucky for us that West did not find a diamond opening lead!

Hand 3 Dealer: West

DUMMY
♠ A 5 3
♥ 7 4 2
♦ J 5
♣ A Q J 8 5

OPENING LEAD:
♠ J

DECLARER (ZIA)
♠ K 8 2
♥ A K J
♦ A K 8 2
♣ K 10 3

NORTH	EAST	SOUTH (Zia)	WEST
			Pass
Pass	Pass	2 NT	Pass
6 NT	Pass	Pass	Pass

It's nice to finish off with a slam contract. We've got eleven sure tricks and it looks as if there are good chances for a twelfth trick but, before we decide what to do, let's go through the steps of the plan.

Solution to Hand 3:

Contract: 6 NT

NORTH
- ♠ A 5 3
- ♥ 7 4 2
- ♦ J 5
- ♣ A Q J 8 5

WEST
- ♠ J 10 9 6
- ♥ Q 10 5
- ♦ Q 7 3
- ♣ 7 4 2

EAST
- ♠ Q 7 4
- ♥ 9 8 6 3
- ♦ 10 9 6 4
- ♣ 9 6

SOUTH
- ♠ K 8 2
- ♥ A K J
- ♦ A K 8 2
- ♣ K 10 3

S   We need to come up with twelve winners to make our slam.

T   We have two sure spade tricks, two sure heart tricks, two sure diamond tricks and five sure club tricks. That's eleven tricks and we need only one more.

O   The obvious place for our extra trick appears to be in the heart suit. If East has the ♥Q, a successful finesse will see us home. Before staking everything on the location of the ♥Q, however, we want to look for other options. The dummy's ♦J gives us a second chance. If West has the ♦Q, we can get a trick by leading towards the dummy's ♦J. Since there are two choices, we'd like to combine them if possible. Does it matter which we try first? Suppose we try the heart finesse first and it loses to West's ♥Q. Now, it is too late to try leading towards the dummy's ♦J. Even if West has the ♦Q, he will win a trick with it and the defence will have two tricks, defeating the contract. Let's try it the other way. If we lead toward the ♦J first and it turns out that East has the ♦Q, we can still fall back on our second chance of the heart finesse. That sounds like a better approach.

P   Having gone through our plan, we now know to win the first trick with the ♠K in our hand and lead a diamond towards the dummy's ♦J. When West wins this trick with the ♦Q, the dummy's ♦J has become our twelfth trick. Careful play

141

has brought in our slam contract, along with the substantial scoring bonus for making it. A nice way to finish. Thank goodness we took time to make our plan before playing to the first trick.

Glossary

Control	Having sufficient trumps or high cards to allow you to keep or get the lead before the opponents can take enough tricks to defeat the contract.
Cover (an honour)	Play a card higher than the previous card played to a trick.
Declarer play	The play of the hand by the declarer, who chooses the cards to play from both his hand and from the dummy.
Dangerous opponent	An opponent who, if he gets the lead, will be able to defeat your contract.
Declarer	The player who first bid the denomination of the final contract. The declarer plays both his cards and the dummy's.
Defeat (contract)	Take enough tricks to prevent the declarer from making his contract.
Develop (tricks)	Play a suit until smaller cards are established or promoted into winners.
Distribution	The shape or pattern of a hand, referring to the number of cards in each suit.
Division	The way a suit is distributed between the two hands of a partnership.
Draw trump	To play the trump suit until the opponents have none left.
Drive out	To play a suit until the opponents are forced to play a higher card than yours in order to win the trick.
Duck	To play a small card to a trick when you could play a higher card to try to win the trick.
Dummy	Declarer's partner. The dummy's hand is placed face up on the table with all the cards exposed and the declarer chooses the cards to be played from the dummy.
Entry	A high card, or trump, which allows the declarer, or the defenders, to get from one hand to another.
Establish (a suit)	Play a suit repeatedly, driving out the opponents' high cards, until your remaining small cards are established as winners.
Finesse	An attempt to win a trick with a high card when a higher card is held by the opponents.
High cards	The ace, king, queen, jack and ten.

Holding	The cards held by a player in a particular suit.
Holdup play	Delay taking the winner(s) in a suit led by the opponents with the objective of making it difficult for the opponents to develop and take their winners in the suit.
Honour (Cards)	The ace, king, queen, jack or ten in a suit.
Location	The hand that contains a specific card.
Long side	The partnership hand containing the most cards in a particular suit.
Losers	Cards in the declarer's hand which may be taken by higher cards held by the opponents.
Overtake	Play a card higher than the one already contributed by your side, even when the original card may win the trick.
Overtrump	Play a trump on a trick that is higher than one played previously.
Plan	Four steps which the declarer can use to guide his play of the hand.
Potential trick	Card that could take a trick after higher cards have been played or if a finesse is successful.
Promotion	Driving out the higher cards held by the opponents in a suit.
Repeated finesse	Take more than one finesse in a suit.
Revoke	Fail to follow suit when you could have done so.
Ruff	Play a trump when you have no cards left in the suit led.
Sequence	Series of touching high cards. For example, the king, queen and jack in a suit make up a sequence.
Short side	The partnership hand with the fewer number of cards in a particular suit.
Side suit	A suit other than the trump suit.
Small cards	Cards below the ten in any suit.
Solid suit	Suit missing no high cards.
Sure trick	A trick which can be taken without giving the lead to the opponents.
Trap a high card	Capture an opponent's high card with the help of a finesse.
Winner	A card which will win a trick when it is played.